THE COMPLETE GUIDE TO MAKING YOUR OWN WINE AT HOME:

Everything You Need to Know Explained Simply

By John N. Peragine Jr.

THE COMPLETE GUIDE TO MAKING YOUR OWN WINE AT HOME: EVERYTHING YOU NEED TO KNOW EXPLAINED SIMPLY

Library of Congress Cataloging-in-Publication Data

Peragine, John N., 1970-
  The complete guide to making your own wine at home : everything you need to know explained simply / John N. Peragine Jr.
    p. cm.
  Includes bibliographical references and index.
  ISBN-13: 978-1-60138-358-7 (alk. paper)
  ISBN-10: 1-60138-358-4 (alk. paper)
  1. Wine and wine making--Amateurs' manual. I. Title.
  TP548.2.P473 2010
  641.8'72--dc22
                              2009051523

Printed in the United States

PROJECT MANAGER: Kim Fulscher • kfulscher@atlantic-pub.com
PEER REVIEWER: Marilee Griffin • mgriffin@atlantic-pub.com
ASSISTANT EDITOR: Angela Pham • apham@atlantic-pub.com
INTERIOR LAYOUT: Antoinette D'Amore • addesign@videotron.ca
FRONT & BACK COVER DESIGN: Jackie Miller • sullmill@charter.net

Printed on Recycled Paper

We recently lost our beloved pet "Bear," who was not only our best and dearest friend but also the "Vice President of Sunshine" here at Atlantic Publishing. He did not receive a salary but worked tirelessly 24 hours a day to please his parents. Bear was a rescue dog that turned around and showered myself, my wife, Sherri, his grandparents Jean, Bob, and Nancy, and every person and animal he met (maybe not rabbits) with friendship and love. He made a lot of people smile every day.

We wanted you to know that a portion of the profits of this book will be donated to The Humane Society of the United States. *–Douglas & Sherri Brown*

The human-animal bond is as old as human history. We cherish our animal companions for their unconditional affection and acceptance. We feel a thrill when we glimpse wild creatures in their natural habitat or in our own backyard.

Unfortunately, the human-animal bond has at times been weakened. Humans have exploited some animal species to the point of extinction.

The Humane Society of the United States makes a difference in the lives of animals here at home and worldwide. The HSUS is dedicated to creating a world where our relationship with animals is guided by compassion. We seek a truly humane society in which animals are respected for their intrinsic value, and where the human-animal bond is strong.

Want to help animals? We have plenty of suggestions. Adopt a pet from a local shelter, join The Humane Society and be a part of our work to help companion animals and wildlife. You will be funding our educational, legislative, investigative and outreach projects in the U.S. and across the globe.

Or perhaps you'd like to make a memorial donation in honor of a pet, friend or relative? You can through our Kindred Spirits program. And if you'd like to contribute in a more structured way, our Planned Giving Office has suggestions about estate planning, annuities, and even gifts of stock that avoid capital gains taxes.

Maybe you have land that you would like to preserve as a lasting habitat for wildlife. Our Wildlife Land Trust can help you. Perhaps the land you want to share is a backyard—that's enough. Our Urban Wildlife Sanctuary Program will show you how to create a habitat for your wild neighbors.

So you see, it's easy to help animals. And The HSUS is here to help.

THE HUMANE SOCIETY
OF THE UNITED STATES.

2100 L Street NW • Washington, DC 20037 • 202-452-1100
www.hsus.org

ACKNOWLEDGMENTS

I dedicate this book to Phil, Kim, Amelia, and Ella: my dear friends and original winemaking inspiration. This also goes to my wife and my two girls, who have tolerated my out-of-control hobby.

TRADEMARK
DISCLAIMER

TABLE OF CONTENTS

CHAPTER 7
COUNTRY WINES   187

CHAPTER 8
MEADS   223

CHAPTER 9
ADDING A CREATIVE TOUCH   247

FOREWORD

Making wine is a fun and fascinating pastime, regardless of how big or small you choose to start. Proximity to California's wine country has given me and my family inspiration to try this hobby, and it has brought many hours of fun and togetherness along the way.

I am fortunate enough to live on a vineyard in California's premier wine-growing region, Napa Valley. I suppose it was almost inevitable that with a ready supply of fruit, I would decide to try my hand at winemaking because I am an enthusiastic home chef and love to experiment with ingredients and techniques.

John Peragine's book gives basic step-by-step instructions on how to create your own wine from fruits and vegetables you might never have considered. While grapes are the standard fruit used in wine; try some of his country recipes if you can't locate a supply of wine grapes right away. The making of non-grape wines has a long and illustrious history in its own right.

Peragine guides you through choosing equipment and ingredients, then takes you through the steps of creating your own wine, from the first grape harvest to the first pour. Home winemaking is what my family does year-round, and we have a history rich in the craft.

When my husband, Frank Hewitt, retired after many years as an engineer for IBM, he and his first wife purchased her mother's property in Napa Valley, which was planted as a prune orchard at the time. Frank and his then-wife, Flossie, wanted to find a retirement lifestyle. Frank began the process of converting the prune orchard to a vineyard by removing the trees and preparing the soil. Long before the time of unsecured loans, his banker insisted that he find a buyer for the yet un-planted grapes before he would grant a loan to plant and develop the property.

In what amounts to a huge stroke of luck, Frank was able to strike up a deal with Christian Brothers winery — one of the leading brands in California's wine industry. They suggested that he plant Cabernet grapes and agreed to buy his crop for ten years. That arrangement allowed him to obtain the loan to plant his first vineyard. All 17 acres under cultivation were laboriously hand-planted by Frank, his wife at the time, and their four children. A true labor of love, it took five years for the vines to be planted, staked, trained, and nurtured before the first crop was picked.

Flossie never saw the project through to completion, as she was tragically killed in a car accident. Frank and his family continued to pursue his dream of retiring as a gentleman farmer. It was a dream he invited me to share with him a few years later, and I joined him in designing and building the home in which we now live. Though it took a number of years before we could move into our new dream home, we have been living here for more than two happy decades, and our family has expanded to include sons- and daughters-in-law along with a slew of grandchildren.

Along the way, Frank and I have had the opportunity to learn firsthand about the winemaking industry from some of the best winemakers in the world. Justin Meyer, founder and winemaker of Silver Oak Cellars and former Christian Brother, was struck by the quality of our vineyard's fruit and the caliber of the young wine. Meyer bought a harvest, and thus began a decades-long relationship with Silver Oak Cellars. The "something special" Justin identified in that 1982 crop became part of the signature of his winemaking style for the next 20 years until his retirement. It helped put his winery on the map and contributed to its recognition by such notable wine writers as Robert Parker of *Wine Spectator*, who described the Cabernet Sauvignon as some of the best coming out of the Napa Valley.

Happily, Justin and his team were more than willing to offer suggestions and guidance when I decided to try making my own wine. His most valuable advice was: "Red wine makes itself." With my family's help, I planted a small row of Merlot along our driveway, and once the grapes were established, I added hundreds of bearded iris and daffodil bulbs. The spring blooms inspired the name of my Merlot, and it has been Purple Iris ever since. Our 26 vines produce between 45 and 60 gallons of wine, all fermented on the wild yeast. This is far more than we can consume ourselves, so I give a large amount of it as gifts to friends and visitors, all of whom are delighted to receive it.

This is all within your reach; this book will explain yeasts, measurements, recipes, fermentation, racking, and all the nuances of home winemaking. When you're ready, you can use Peragine's information on how to start your own winery, the regulations you will need to follow, how to grow your own grapes, and tips on how to label your own wine.

Both my Cabernet and Merlot wines have won numerous awards at state and county fairs. Even the labels have won prizes, thanks to my eldest daughter's training as a graphic artist. These days, my winemaking team includes my youngest daughter and her husband, who have also been bitten by the bug. Together with their willing and enthusiastic friends, we pick, crush, ferment, and bottle the wines that accompany many of our family meals. I take pride in being able to pass along what I've learned to a new team of home winemakers. A special section of this book includes photos of our team harvesting and crushing the grapes, pouring the wine, and enjoying the vineyards.

While a lot of the history of my family's vineyard has been due to good fortune, none of that luck would have happened if the grapes themselves hadn't been of the quality to attract such positive attention. The lesson is: Use only the best ingredients. Whether you are making wine from grapes or wine from any of the other fruit in the recipes in this book, your wine will only be as good as what you put into it. And remember: Winemaking is a natural process. One of the hardest lessons I've learned is to step back and let my wine make itself.

While I don't recommend starting off with a 60-gallon barrel as your first attempt at winemaking, I think it's safe to say that if you do your research and trust your instincts, you will soon join the ranks of other enthusiastic home winemakers.

Skaal! *(Cheers!)*

Inger Hewitt
Hewitt Family Vineyard
Napa Valley, California

INTRODUCTION

Benefits of Making Wine At Home

> "A typical wine writer was once described as someone with a typewriter who was looking for his name in print, a free lunch, and a way to write off his wine cellar. It's a dated view. Wine writers now use computers."
>
> — Frank Prial, *The New York Times*; January 21, 1998

There is a craft that is thousands of years old. Both an industry and a hobby, families, villages, communities, and entire cultures engage in winemaking. Wine is so precious to the French that during World War II, the French hid their wines in caves during the Nazi invasion. Wine, at its most basic, is the fermentation of a fruit juice or other sweet liquid. The natural yeasts found on the skins of the fruit and in the air utilize the sugar as food, producing alcohol. From an accident of nature, one of the most diverse beverages known to mankind has evolved.

Wine has been the theme of love poems and songs, and made men and women strong in legends. The history and importance of wine is fascinating, and even today it plays a central role in many religions, cultures, beliefs, and commerce.

Unless there are laws forbidding it, you can go to just about any store or restaurant and find wine. It is almost as common as water, and the variations of flavors, colors, aromas, and even price are endless. The main ingredient in wine, the grape, is grown on nearly every continent in the world. It is a hardy vine that can grow in even the most unfavorable agricultural conditions.

I had always assumed creating wine, even great wine, was something that could only be done in a factory or specialty winery. I never imagined that I could not only create wine in my own home, but that the creations were as good as or even better than commercial offerings.

In North Carolina, there are a number of different wineries. As tobacco crops have been in less demand, many farmers have turned their land over to grape growing. There are many small wineries that dot the North Carolina and Virginia landscapes and in the Yadkin Valley, where vintners have found prime growing conditions for many types of American vines.

One of the most spectacular of these wineries, the Biltmore Estate, located in Asheville, North Carolina, is tucked away in the Blue Ridge Mountains. The Biltmore Estate's winery was created out of a dairy barn and has been one of the estate's main forms of income since 1985. I have been making wines at home for a number of years, but I learned even more when I visited the estates in August 2009 because I was able to go on a behind-the-scenes tour and was inspired to try new techniques and create some wines I had not tried in a while. Even on the large scale like the one at the

Biltmore Estate, the techniques and processes of creating wine are the same as those you would use at home.

The next step was buying basic winemaking equipment, purchasing a wine book, and getting to work. It has been 18 years since I started making wine, and my house and rented storage space are full of wine, empty wine bottles, and equipment. My wife has been tolerant because she loves the new wines I create for her to try. Every Christmas, I always have the perfect gifts to give to family and friends.

I warn you: Once you start making your own wine, you will not be able to stop. The basic process is simple, but the subtle variations in ingredients, maturation time, and other variables that are involved in the winemaking process are what give wine its intrigue. Every batch of wine you create will take on a character and life of its own.

In these times of economic uncertainty, isn't it nice to know that you can create world-class wine in the privacy of your own home for about $2 a bottle? The price can vary depending on the ingredients, but making your own wine is not an overly expensive hobby. Once you buy the basic equipment, all you will need to buy are the ingredients. All of the recipes included in this book will create either 1 gallon or 5 gallons of wine, though each of the 1-gallon recipes can be adapted to create 5 gallons. Five gallons of wine will make approximately 25 average-sized 750-ml. wine bottles.

Making wine is a social hobby. It is one that you can include friends and family in during the process. I have been a part of different winemaking clubs around the area I live in. Being a member of such a group helps to cut down on the cost of making larger batches of wine and helps defray the cost of purchasing more advanced — and more expensive — equipment.

IS WINEMAKING LEGAL?

"A man will be eloquent if you give him good wine."

— Ralph Waldo Emerson, *Representative Men*

Until 1979, it was not legal to produce wine at home without a permit. The federal government waived that requirement, but there are still a few restrictions. You can produce 100 gallons of wine per person, or 200 gallons of wine a year per household, without a permit. If you are bitten by the winemaking bug and want to produce more, you will need the appropriate permits from your state's Alcoholic Beverage Commission (ABC) that is the governing body that a winemaker must apply to. Each state may have different rules and applications; in order to find your state's ABC, type your state's name and "Alcoholic Beverage Commission" into a search engine.

Do not worry that you are limited by the 200-gallon limit. Consider that 5 gallons of wine produces 25 standard 750-ml. bottles; therefore, 200 gallons of wine will produce 1,000 bottles of wine. You would have to drink almost three bottles of wine a day for a year to consume that much wine. If you create a 5-gallon batch every month or two, you will produce 300 bottles of wine a year, which is nowhere near the 1,000-bottle limit.

Throughout this book, I have provided some 1-gallon recipes; it gives you the chance to produce more varieties of wine without having to move out of your home or dig a large wine cellar. Besides, producing 100 gallons of wine can get expensive. It will feel less wasteful to dump 1 gallon of wine than to dump 5 gallons. Every home winemaker I have ever met has more than one story of a failed batch of homemade wine. It comes with the territory.

A BRIEF HISTORY OF WINEMAKING

The process of creating wine is a relatively simple one. In fact, spontaneous fermentation of fruit juice happens all the time without human intervention. There are many different stories about how winemaking first began, but none are confirmable. One of the theories is that juice or some other fermentable sugar, such as honey, found its way into water. This could have occurred after a rainstorm, in which the honey and water mixture sat. Wild yeasts took over and created a natural brew.

Who was the brave soul who first tried a natural wine? What did it taste like? Was it the result of a dare? Someone may have used their hands to scoop up the brew and probably experienced the world's first hangover. For whatever reason, someone actually tried it a second time, and winemaking has been an integral part of man's culture and history ever since.

Winemaking is quite ancient and reaches back to Neolithic times. During the period when man began to domesticate plants and animals and civilization began, formerly nomadic cultures settled in fertile regions and began growing crops. While fermentation was doubtless discovered and encouraged prior to the development of clay vessels, serious winemaking required large-scale means of storage.

In 1968, archaeologist Mary M. Voigt excavated a site in the Zagros Mountains of Iran, where she discovered a yellow residue in the bottom of a jar. The jar was big enough to hold about 9 liters (2.5 gallons) and was located with five other jars in the area of a structure that was thought to be a kitchen. In 1996, when technology became available to analyze such residues, it was confirmed the residue was, in fact, wine. This ancient wine was named Chateau Hajji Firuz and dated circa 5400 to 5000 BC.

Domesticated grape plants were transplanted in the mid-3rd century BCE throughout Europe, Asia, and Africa. There are Assyrian reliefs that show men and women lounging under grape arbors and drinking what could be inferred to be wine.

Since these ancient beginnings, winemaking continues to be a regular practice around the world and touches nearly every continent and culture. You will learn these ancient techniques and create wines your family and friends will love. The problem will be making enough to keep up with the demand.

Following are further interesting facts about some of the ways wine has figured into history:

- The United States' third president, Thomas Jefferson, stocked the Presidential wine cellars so full that the contents lasted through the first five U.S. presidents. His favorite wines were Bordeaux and Madeira.

- Around 1300 BC in Egypt (the time of King Tut), the common people drank beer while the upper class drank wine.

- Fermented beverages have been consumed far more often than water until recent history because they were usually safer and more sanitary than the water supply.

- In 1001 AD, Viking Leif Ericson landed in North America and was impressed by the number of grapevines, so he named the new land "Vinland," or in the English translation, "Wineland."

- In 4000 BCE, the Egyptians used corks as stoppers, but it was not until late 17th century they were used as a way to stop a bottle so they could be laid to age. It was also when the shape of wine bottles began to evolve from short, bulbous bottles to tall, slender ones.

- In 79 AD, Mount Vesuvius erupted and buried Pompeii — along with about 200 wine bars.

Wine has played a large role in the establishment, history, and commerce of the United States. In fact, American wine has been produced commercially for more than 300 years. Today, wine is made and sold in all 50 states. California, Washington state, Oregon, and New York are the leading wine-growing regions. If you live in these areas, you are fortunate because you will find more places to buy supplies and fresh grapes to produce wine at home, as well as many wine clubs.

The United States has the distinction of being the fourth-largest wine-producing country, just behind France, Italy, and Spain. The state of California creates more wine annually than does the continent of Australia. When the first Europeans visited the United

States, they found several native grape species already growing there, among which are:

- *Vitis labrusca* (Concord grape)
- *Vitis riparia* (Riverbank or Frost grape)
- *Vitis rotundifolia* (Muscadines)
- *Vitis aestivalis* (Summer grape)
- *Vitis californica* (California grape)

These vines can still be found growing wild and under cultivation in different places around the United States, but the wine industry was really born in the United States when *Vitis vinifera* was introduced. In Virginia and the Carolinas, the industry flourished in the early colonies and was a main crop and source of revenue.

Vitis vinifera, or the common European wine grape, originated in the Old World. This vine has been developed into the varietals that are usually used today in modern winemaking. Some examples of varietals are Merlot, Chardonnay, and Pinot Grigio, among many others.

The native varieties of grape, while good, were not pleasing to the European palate. So the Virginia Company began exporting French vinifera vines to Virginia in 1619. However, these French vines were afflicted with insects and disease when planted in American soil. In 1683, William Penn planted a vineyard of French vinifera in Pennsylvania that may have interbred with a native *Vitis labrusca* vine to create the hybrid grape Alexander.

The first commercial vineyard and winery in the United States was established by an act of the Kentucky Legislature on November 21, 1799. The vinedresser for the vineyard was John James Dufour, formerly of Vevey, Switzerland. The vineyard was located overlooking the Kentucky River in Jessamine County, Kentucky, and was named First Vineyard by Dufour. Two 5-gallon oak casks of wine were taken to President Thomas Jefferson in Washington, D.C. The vineyard continued until 1809, when a killing freeze in May destroyed the crop and many vines at the First Vineyard. The Dufour family then relocated to Vevay in Switzerland County, Indiana, and planted a new vineyard with the Alexander grape.

Grape growing in California was established in the late 1700s by Franciscan missionary Junipero Serra, and vines were carried northward by later missionaries. The vinifera varietal used was the Mission grape, one of admittedly modest quality. Winemaking continued to advance and improve in the West under the Spanish.

Wineries and vineyards flourished and grew across the United States through the late 1800s, when a combination of factors ranging from the phylloxera epidemic in the West and Pierce's disease in the East ravaged the growing American wine industry. Cuttings of American grapes taken to botanical gardens in Britain brought with them the phylloxera root louse, which spread throughout Europe, destroying most of the producing vineyards. Thomas Munson, a horticulturist in Texas, suggested grafting the European vinifera vines onto American riparia rootsocks. This began the long, laborious process of grafting every wine vine in Europe over to American rootstocks. It was the only way that the European wine industry could be salvaged. It was also this grafting technique that provides today's wine grapes in America with desirable disease-resistance.

When Maine became the first dry state in 1846, meaning alcohol was illegal for sale or production, the result was a growing, nationwide prohibition movement. The 1920 passage of the Eighteenth Amendment to the U.S. Constitution stated that it was illegal to manufacture, sell, or transport alcohol, and essentially killed the wine industry in America. The only exception to this new law was sacramental wine. This was the period of the speakeasy and bathtub gin, and many people flagrantly violated the law. It was during this time that home-winemaking began to take hold as families made wine for personal consumption under the auspices of the constitutional exclusion of sacramental wine production.

By the time prohibition was lifted in 1933, the wine industry in the United States was in shambles. The old winemakers had passed away, and vineyards had died. The grapes that were left made what was referred to as table wines. Americans now wanted cheaper wine, sometimes called "Dago Red," and sweeter, fortified wines. Their tastes had changed, and only the traditionalist home winemakers still made the Old World wines, which refer to European vinifera varietals.

Over the next 40 years, the wine industry in America got back on its feet. However, it was not until the mid-1970s that American winemaking became internationally known. The May 24, 1976 blind-tasting held in Paris comprised a panel of French wine experts. After comparing six California Chardonnays with four French Chardonnays, the panelists selected three California wines out of the top four. The upset win brought in foreign financial backing, and a winemaking boom occurred in the late 1970s and 1980s. In 2004, 668 million gallons of wine were created for consumers in the United States alone — and those numbers continue to grow every year.

As American tastes have become more sophisticated, more people are looking for the wines made from the Old World varietals. Some of them are very expensive, and this is how home winemaking has found its niche. You can produce any kind of wine you want at home for a fraction of what it costs in a store. You can choose from hundreds of different kinds of grapes and juices. You can press and crush grapes yourself, or you can buy wine kits that contain everything, including crushed, pressed, and filtered grape juice. If you are lucky, you might find a local wine- and beer-making hobby shop in the yellow pages. *These wine kits can be purchased from online sources mentioned in Appendix D of this book.*

In this book, you will learn the basics of making wine at home. You will be amazed at how simple it is and, like me, you may wonder why you did not start sooner. My family is from Italy and Ireland, and there was never a shortage of wine on the dinner table or as part of holiday celebrations. My immediate family produces wine for our own personal consumption, but we also know some families who produced enough for their extended families or even their communities to share. I now hand down this tradition to you to enjoy with your family and friends.

Sit, relax, and enjoy a home-crafted glass of wine.

CHAPTER 1

Wine: Start at the Beginning

> "Making good wine is a skill; making fine wine is an art."
> — Robert Mondavi, world-famous winemaker

Wine is the amazing combination of the right amounts of water, sugar, and yeast. It is important to understand how these three basic elements make wine.

It does not matter if you decide to make a Chardonnay, a Merlot, or a Cabernet — the process that the wine undergoes remains the same. Even country wines that use fruits or vegetables also undergo the same fermentation process. The only thing that may change is the type of sugar, water, or yeast. The flavors and smells of the fruit being used add to the flavor and bouquet of the wine, but the actual process of making wine from grapes or any fruit remains unchanged.

There is fancier equipment to help refine your wine and make it clearer and have a cleaner taste, but the actual process of fermentation is one that occurs naturally. You can control the temperature, give the yeast a boost, and even kill off the yeast when it is complete, but in order to transform fruit juice into wine, you must allow the yeast to digest and metabolize sugar. There is no other synthetic process that can duplicate it.

The process goes something like this: Water is the chief constituent of all fruit juices. As you will learn, the pretty, ruby-colored wine you love to drink is created by live yeast. Water is essential because yeast needs it in order to thrive. Water is also the universal solvent, so it provides a medium for the yeast to have access to the sugar that is dissolved within the liquid.

Yeast is a microorganism in the fungus family. It is used in all fermented products — from breads, beer, and wine to pastries. It works to make things expand and rise by metabolizing carbohydrates (sugar) and in the process creating carbon dioxide gas. In the case of wine, the second by-product of digestion is ethanol.

Yeast loves sugar and uses it for most of its biological functions; it eats, grows, procreates, and dies. It is through the biological process of living that yeast transforms sugar into alcohol. There are some lengthy biological and chemical reactions that occur, but knowing just the basic process is sufficient in creating world-class wine.

Yeast consumes sugar because it is essential to its metabolic processes. Yeast metabolism is not very different from the human digestion process. When we digest food, we also transform it into a different form, whether it is gas, liquid, or solid. We draw energy from the sugar we eat, and our bodies excrete what we do not need. In the case of yeast, it excretes alcohol and gas. The gas is in the form of little tiny bubbles. You can find those same bubbles in Champagne. They are composed of carbon dioxide, which is the same gas humans expel when breathing. This process of yeast metabolism is essential to understand because without the right balances of ingredients and conditions, such as temperature, the yeast cannot thrive. If you have ever owned fish and a fish tank, you know that the right combination of temperature, food, and water is important. If there is too much food, not enough air in the tank, or the temperature is too high or low, the fish will die. Yeast is not so very different. In the next section, you will learn what the right water, food source, and types of yeast are available for winemaking.

THE ESSENTIAL THREE

Winemaking is simple because you only need three things to accomplish it, and all of them can be found in nature. Our ancient ancestors believed the wines just "happened" — it was something the Gods and nature spirits created, and it was shrouded in mystery. Over the centuries, the knowledge of the process of winemaking has boiled down the ingredients to three vital elements: water, sugar, and yeast.

The primary fermentation converts sugar to alcohol. Once the wine reaches a certain level of alcohol, the yeast will die and the process of fermentation will cease. In some cases, not all the yeast dies, but it is instead left in a state of suspended animation. You have seen this state if you have ever opened a packet of yeast to make bread. It is dried and visually lifeless until water is added to it. Wine yeast comes in the same kind of packets bread yeast does.

> **TIP** Never use bread yeast to make wine. You will regret the decision and will quickly pour it down the drain. Bread yeast will leave a bad aftertaste in your wine. It is great at leavening bread, but it is not so great at creating alcohol.

If the temperature of the wine rises and there is a sufficient amount of residual sugar, this yeast can come back to life. For a home winemaker, this is akin to creating liquid hand grenades. The corks and bottles will literally explode and redecorate part of your house all the way to the ceiling. Though not generally desirable for the home winemaker, secondary fermentation is often deliberately encouraged by adding a second type of yeast to commercially produced wines in order to convert maltose sugar to lactose. In the wine industry, this in known as malolactic fermentation, and is the conversion of L-malic acid to L-lactic acid. This gives some California Chardonnays their characteristic buttery mouth-feel, but is not a good thing in more fruit-forward white varieties like Sauvignon Blanc. Malolactic fermentation is also encouraged in many red wine varieties to reduce the likelihood of just such explosive bottle-grenades.

I will give you tips throughout this book on how to avoid this, although if you make wine for long enough, this will probably happen at least once. Just be prepared, and do not place your bottled wine or fermentation vessel next to any nice furniture.

I once created raspberry mead, a honey-based wine, and placed the bottles in my dining room. While I was watching television about a week later, there was a popping sound. It was not loud, but it sounded like popcorn beginning to pop in a microwave. I went to investigate, and there was pink liquid dripping from the ceiling. That was quite a mess to clean up. As you will learn later in the book, you must make sure the wine has stopped fermenting before you bottle it.

If you combine the three essential ingredients, you can create just about any kind of wine. The sugars in wine are sucrose and glucose.

You cannot use artificial sweeteners to create wine, which is why you will never find sugar-free or diet wine. Sugar combined with alcohol gives you the perception of sweetness in wine. In dry wines, the yeast consumes most of the sugar before fermentation ends, and in sweet wines the yeast will die off before consuming all the available sugar. The natural acids found in fruit, or acid additives that are added to the wine, create the acid taste in wine. One of the most common acids used in wine is citric acid.

Phenols, a chemical compound naturally found in food and similar to alcohols, create the bitter taste in wine usually in the form of tannins. Tannins are a type of phenol that has the property of shrinking proteins and is what gives red wine its astringent taste. There are more tannins in red wines than white. Currently, scientists are researching the health benefits of wine in more than a dozen studies, and phenols are the most promising component under scrutiny.

Most plants contain some amount of sugar, as it is needed for growth and energy. Fruit, the result of the pollination of flowers, contains more sugars than other parts of a plant and are therefore sweeter. Any plant can be used to create wine, although some are much tastier to use than others.

In addition to water, sugar, and yeast, there are different chemicals that can be added to stop fermentation and make wine clearer or more stable. These do not add much to the taste of the wine; however, they are essential to certain chemical processes that are necessary in creating a clear and clean-tasting wine.

It is the manipulation of the three essential ingredients that make each wine unique and different. Let us take a look at each of these ingredients in more detail, as they are the basis of creating any wine.

Wine is made up of 95 percent water and alcohol. The other 5 percent is made up of various compounds that give wine its many possible flavor variations. More than 1,000 different compounds can be found in wine.

WATER

Water is essential to all life, and it is also essential to your wine. Different regions around the world create a one-of-a-kind taste in their wine, beer, and liquor just because of the water they use. You may not think water has an actual taste, but it does. There are trace minerals that affect the taste, and they are also important for a healthy fermentation.

Not all water is created the same. Water comes from a number of different sources:

- Tap water
- Spring water
- Well water
- Distilled water
- Bottled drinking water

Tap water

Where you live determines the source and quality of your tap water. There is a wide range of tap water and, just like Goldilocks, you must find the one that is just right.

This water is too hard

Hard water is full of minerals such as calcium, magnesium, and other metals. This type of water leaves deposits on pipes and spots on dishes and kitchen utensils. You can do a simple test to determine if your water is hard. Try to create lather with some soap and water. Hard water will not easily create or maintain foam. Generally, the pH of hard water is alkaline; this can leave a bitter taste in the water, and therefore in your wine. If you consider softening your water with a water treatment system, you should be aware this will make the wine taste salty and unpleasant.

> **TIP** Do not use softened water to make wine. You should avoid using hard water and move on to other more palatable water choices. Besides being salty, the process of softening water will remove essential minerals needed for a healthy fermentation.

This water is too soft

On the other end of the spectrum is soft water, which contains fewer minerals and is the best selection if you choose to use tap water. Soft water is not perfect; it tends to be more acidic and leaches metals into your wine. This can give your wine a metallic or sour taste. Taste your water first and determine if these characteristics exist before destroying a potentially good wine.

This water is just right

Relatively pH-neutral (a pH of approximately 7.0) water with sufficient minerals is a good choice. You can test your water's pH at home using a water-testing kit. For about $20, you can purchase a water-testing kit at **www.air-n-water.com**, or you can send it off to be tested at a county, state, or private lab. You can call your county's environmental agency for suggestions.

Some water supplies have a high amount of chlorine or have been fluoridated. This can cause an off-taste to your wine. Briefly boiling your water can help release these gases without losing minerals in your water, but be careful not to over-boil it. You can also pass your water through an activated charcoal filter.

Spring water

Many homes in rural areas use spring water for their drinking water. This is the best water you can use because it contains everything you want as far as minerals but does not contain any added chemicals, such as chlorine. If you buy gallons of spring water from the store, make sure it is really spring water and not tap water. Look at the label to confirm that it is ozonized and that it is not from a municipal water supply. Tap water from another city is not bad; it is just not spring water. If you see on the label of a bottled water of any kind that it has been ozonized, this means no chemicals were used to kill any bacteria in the water.

Well water

Well water is different from spring water because it often contains iron and other metals. This makes it hard water, as described above. You can try to pass it through an activated charcoal filter, but there still may be some disagreeable flavors that would not make a good choice for wine.

Distilled water

I like to refer to distilled water as "dead water." All the water's living components and minerals are removed during the distillation process. You can buy distilled water at the store or create it at home by boiling and evaporating water. When the water condenses, it is distilled. But yeast cannot survive and reproduce in this kind of environment, so avoid using this type of processed water.

Bottled water

Many designer bottled water brands contain minerals and additives, such as salt, in an attempt to make their water more palatable. Read the labels and make sure you do not see any mention of minerals and additives — if you see them, you should avoid them. There are some brands you can buy that do not contain many additives. When I lived in a house that had bad-tasting tap water, I bought the grocery store brand of spring water. It was cheap and worked wonderfully: I won three wine competitions while using that bottled water.

Never use flavored waters or fitness water. I cannot even describe what it would taste like, and it is unlikely you will ever get yeast to live in it.

When making wine from grapes, it is not as essential to add water because the fruit has plenty of liquid. In fact, water is usually used to dilute the wine only if the pH or specific gravity is off. If you are creating wines with plants and fruits other than grapes, the addition of water is much more important. When you are using different parts of a plant like the stems, leaves, or even roots, the wine needs more water because these parts do not usually contain as much liquid.

Wine must — This is a term to describe the fermenting grape juice as yeast is converting sugars into carbon dioxide and alcohol.

SUGAR

Wine, in this instance, is considered to be the fermentation product of any sugar solution, from grape juice to extractions of grains or flowers or other plant materials. Generally, fruit juices will not require the addition of significant amounts of additional sugar, while other plant materials will necessitate varying additions of sugar to produce the desired result.

Sugar is a term that can mean different types of chemical compounds. The three forms of sugar humans most often consume are glucose, fructose, and sucrose. The most common form of sugar is sucrose in a crystallized form — also known as common white sugar — which is created from sugar cane or sugar beets. Fructose is a type of sugar found in fruit and corn, and glucose is a base sugar only found in conjunction with fructose and sucrose. Besides white sugar and plant sources, sugar can also be found in high concentrations in syrups such as honey, maple syrup, or molasses.

Sugar in its natural form has a tan color and a molasses flavor. Using the more natural forms of sugar to sweeten your wine or raise the potential alcohol level will make your wine darker and give it a slight molasses taste. If you are creating a wine for your vegan friends, you may consider using raw sugar.

White sugar is processed; some sugar companies use bone char from cattle to remove the color from the sugar. This is why vegans do not eat processed sugar. Some sugar companies add activated charcoal to the process to remove the charred bone after it has bleached the sugar.

Heating bones to about 400 to 500 degrees Celsius creates bone char. The result is a black material that is used in filters to clean aquariums and remove fluoride from water, as well as in the process of creating petroleum jelly from crude oil, and is a pigment often sometimes used by painters to create a deep black color. The sugar is passed through the bone char, which absorbs the caramel color and leaves it white.

Using white sugar is fine, but be careful how much you add to wine. You can always add more sugar to wine, but you can never take any out. Using too much white sugar can impart a cider taste to your wine. Adding sugar to wine to increase the alcohol content of wine is referred to as "chapitalization," and there are many wine-producing areas around the world that have strict laws concerning this practice.

The chapitalization process is not intended to make the wine sweeter; it is only to give it a higher alcohol content. This practice began in areas where the grapes had a lower initial sugar content. These rules against adding sugar to sweeten wine exist in places like Italy and California. This keeps a certain standard of quality to the wine in these regions. However, winemakers are allowed to use grape juice concentrate to add sweetness. In making wine at home, sometimes the wine needs more sugar to produce a specific taste or to fix an overly dry wine.

Normally, you would use white cane sugar in your wines. Grapes usually contain their own sugars for alcohol conversion and taste and therefore will not often require additional sugar. You are not limited to just using those sugars. The following is a list of different sugars to experiment with. Try one at a time and in small batches, as some of these experiments may not be pleasing to the palate.

Bar sugar: This is the king of granulated sugars. It is also referred to as "ultrafine," "superfine," or, in England, as "caster sugar." In specialty food stores it is often sold as "baker's sugar."

Barbados sugar: This is a very dark type of brown sugar. It will impart a stronger molasses flavor and darker color to your wine. It is also known as muscovado sugar. You can find this in most ethnic food sections in the grocery store.

Brown sugar: This should not be confused with raw sugar. Brown sugar has molasses syrup added to enhance the sugar's color and flavor. The difference between light and dark brown sugar is the amount of molasses that is added to the white sugar. If you use brown sugar, you should stick with the lighter brown sugar, as the dark brown sugar can overwhelm the flavor of your wine.

Corn syrup: Corn syrup is mostly made of glucose and water. Some corn syrups may have other sugars or even a vanilla flavor added. Read the ingredients on the label, as some additives could hurt your fermentation. If vanilla has been added, this could make a strange off-taste to your wine and should be avoided. *See glucose.*

Demerara sugar: This is a type of light brown sugar, but with the consistency of large, sticky crystals. This is a premium sugar; it is hard to find and rather expensive. You may want to try it in some of your recipes for a unique touch. You might find this online or in baking specialty shops.

Dextrose: This is a type of glucose found in most fruits and honey. You will not find this as something you can buy; it is mentioned here as a natural sugar in foods.

Fructose: This type of sugar can be found in a variety of fruit, and is usually found paired with glucose. Fructose is much sweeter in taste than glucose, and fruits high in fructose tend to make sweeter wines. Usually people use fructose found naturally in foods. You may be able to purchase fructose in health food stores and larger grocery stores.

Galactose: This is another type of glucose and is sometimes called lactose. You should not use this in winemaking, as it will oxidize and form mucic acid.

Grape juice concentrate: Readily available at most grocery stores, this is what professional winemakers use in the event that there is not enough naturally occurring sugar in their fruit; it eliminates the need for refined sugar.

Glucose: This is the other type of sugar, along with fructose, that is found naturally in fruit. It is fermentable but not as sweet as fructose. You cannot purchase glucose in stores because it occurs naturally in some foods. *See corn syrup.*

Honey: The average composition of honey is glucose (in the form of dextrose; constitutes about 30 percent of the honey), fructose (in the form of levulose; constitutes about 38 to 40 percent), maltose (about 7 percent), and some other sugars, depending on the variety. Honey may also contain water, bee parts, mineral, minerals, pollens, and other solids. The variety of honey is controlled by what flowers are available to the bees that create it. Some varieties are wildflower, locust, orange blossom, clover, and heather. There are many different varieties of honey, and they vary in color, sweetness, and composition. Honey is used as a fermentable sugar or as a sweetener in wines along with other fruits. If honey is used as the primary sugar and flavor in a wine, then the wine is referred to as mead.

Invert sugar: This is type of sugar is created through the process of converting sucrose to glucose and fructose. The forms sugar takes when it is inverted are dextrose (a type of glucose) and levulose (type of fructose). Yeast can more readily use inverted sugar because it does not have to break down sucrose itself. You can create inverted sugar yourself by putting two parts sugar into one part water. Mix 2 teaspoons of lemon juice for every 1 pound of sugar (which is about 2 ¼ cups of granulated sugar). Bring this mixture to a point close to boiling for 30 minutes. Do not allow the mixture to actually boil. You should use it immediately or place in a sealed jar in the refrigerator. Do not use the inverted sugar to sweeten wine; it might re-ferment, which can result in exploding bottles or a strong alcohol-tasting wine.

Jaggery: This is a type of palm sugar that is produced in the East Indies and is created by evaporating the fresh juice of several kinds of palm trees. It is in a raw or slightly processed form. You can find this in many ethnic markets.

Maltose: This type of sugar is created from starch, specifically malt, and is processed using amylolytic fermentation. This is the same reaction that occurs when saliva or pancreatic juices are introduced to a starch. You can experience this by chewing a cracker; eventually, it will turn sweet in your mouth. This can be found in small amounts in certain types of sugar and honey.

Molasses: This is the liquid part of sugar that is left after the crystallized portion has been removed. There are different grades of molasses. The lighter the grade, the more sugar it contains. For instance, light molasses contains 90 percent sugar, while "blackstrap molasses" contains only 50 percent sugar; the rest is refinement residue. Because of sulfur compounds that are added to molasses, it is not usually recommended to use in winemaking because it can create an undesirable odor and flavor. There are some recipes that call for small amounts, but this is generally for a type of flavor rather than for fermentation purposes.

Piloncillo: This type is a granulated, slightly refined brown sugar from Mexico that you can buy in cone-shaped cakes. This is a more natural sugar and tastes different than other brown sugars, which have molasses added to refined sugar. Piloncillo is more like raw sugar. This can be found in the ethnic food section of most well-stocked supermarkets.

Raffinose: This complex carbohydrate sugar is found in grains, legumes, and some root vegetables. It is only slightly sweet, but can add a distinct flavor. It cannot be purchased, but it can be found in the previously mentioned foods.

Raw sugar: This is unrefined sugar created by the evaporation of cane, beet, maple, or some other syrup. It is also known as Sucanat®. This can be readily found in most major supermarkets.

Residual sugar: This is a term to refer to the sugar that is left after fermentation has halted in a wine, which occurs one of two ways:

1. The yeast has converted all the available fermentable sugar. There may be sugar left in the wine, but this residual sugar is not fermentable.

2. The alcohol level has reached such a toxic level in the wine that the yeast dies. This toxicity level depends on the yeast strain being used. There may be both fermentable and non-fermentable sugars left in the wine.

Rock candy: This type of sugar comes in large crystals made of sucrose and is clear in color. The crystals can be tinted different colors due to added flavorings. Some home winemakers place a piece of rock candy in the bottom of a wine bottle before filling it, which allows the sugar to slowly dissolve and sweeten the wine.

Stachyose: This is a complex sugar that can be found in grains, legumes, and some other vegetables. It is less sweet than raffinose, and does not work very well as a fermentable sugar or as a sweetener. It does impart a unique flavor in certain kinds of wine that are made with other fruits and vegetables other than grapes.

Sucrose: This is what regular white granulated sugar is made of and what is commonly used in winemaking. It is naturally found in grapes, fruit, and many other plants. Granulated sugar is made from refining sugar cane, sugar beets, and other sugar sources. This can be added directly to wine must. It must be broken down and inverted by the yeast into fructose and glucose before it can be used for fermentation.

Treacle: This is a refinement residue very similar to molasses; however, treacle is generally darker. Black treacle is very similar in taste to blackstrap molasses. It does not contain the sulfur that molasses does, so it is much better to use in winemaking.

Experiment with sugars and see what kinds of flavors you can come up with. Try these types of sugar in small 1-gallon batches, because you may want to pour some of it down the drain. You may want to try using the sugar with the fruits first in a smoothie. If you hate the combination of flavors, it will not improve much as a wine.

YEAST

Because our ancestors did not understand the concept of micro-organisms, they were not sure how fermentation worked. They knew that leaving out fruit juice over time would lead to the formation of wine, but to them it was a magical process. They would place crushed fruit in large, open vessels, and the wild yeast would begin fermentation on its own. It is likely that many of these early batches were mostly vinegar, but over time humans discovered microorganisms such as bacteria and yeasts.

To our ancestors, this process was so mystical that they felt the secrets of fermentation belonged to the gods and goddesses of their culture. The ancient Romans would hold great festivals in honor of the god Bacchus, called Bacchanals. These festivals were celebrated for days and sometimes weeks during the harvest of grapes and the creation of wine.

Winemaking is an organic, living process rather than a set of chemical reactions that can be reproduced in a chemistry lab. There are chemical reactions that happen within the yeast cells, but it is a digestive process that cannot occur simply by mixing together chemicals. There is no way around it; you need live yeast cells to create any fermented product. Like water and sugar, there are different types of yeast. As mentioned, you should not use baker's yeast, the kind used to leaven bread. It will make your wine taste like liquid bread.

Yeast live naturally on the skin of fruits such as grapes, blueberries, and plums. It is the whitish color that can often be found on wild varieties of these fruits. You can make wine by just crushing fruit and allowing the wild yeast to take over. The results are unpredictable, though, and you risk contamination by other microorganisms. This was the way our predecessors made wine, by stomping the fruit and allowing it to ferment naturally. Some wineries still use wild fermentation to create their wines.

TIP Some wines are created in open vats, and there are wineries and brew houses that have been making wine and beer this way for centuries. Every nook, cranny, wall, floor board, and implement in these structures contain particular strains of yeast, so open-vat fermentation is easier to accomplish. The wines produced in these unique structures cannot be duplicated elsewhere, because the particular strains only exist in these places. If you are fortunate enough to live in a wine-producing area, consider experimenting with wild yeast if you have access to freshly picked wine grapes. Wild yeasts tend to be specifically evolved to match the grape variety they live on and can produce excellent results. While they may not be as vigorous as commercial yeasts, they can impart a subtlety lacking in purchased yeast. Because they may be a bit slower to consume the grape sugars, keeping your fermentation vessel slightly warmer than room temperature will help them along.

These little microscopic creatures live to do one thing — eat — and the only food on their menu is sugar. Wine yeast usually comes freeze-dried in small packets, which can be purchased from a winemaking supply store. When the wine must is ready, the packet is emptied into the juice mixture. The water reconstitutes them, and they are ready to go. Within a few hours, they will eat, release gas, produce alcohol, and procreate. The next generation will begin to do the same as the parent yeast dies off. This dead yeast will sink to the bottom of the bucket. When you make wine for the first time, you will see this brown sludge, which is called "lees." *A list of stores around the United States and other online resources can be found in Appendix D of this book.*

After the yeast dies off and the lees are visible, you will go through a process called "racking." This is a process of drawing the clear wine off the top of the lees while trying not to disturb the sediment. There are a number of different ways this can be accomplished, but the most common is by using tubing and siphoning the wine into another sanitized container. There are some particles that are not removed. Therefore, when you drink your favorite Pinot Grigio, you also taste yeast. They contribute to the complexity of the wine and actually add some trace amounts of protein. Thus, picking the right yeast does matter.

There are three basic types of yeast — some for white wines, some for red wines, and others you can use for any kind of wine. The choice of yeast helps determine not only the complexity of the taste of a particular wine, but also its alcohol content. There are many different brands and variations of yeast to choose from. *A list of the most common types can be found in Appendix A.*

You can use dry yeast for any kind of wine. Sometimes it can be tough to get the yeast stimulated enough to start fermentation, and you might have to create a yeast culture. To encourage it to divide and begin fermentation, mix your dry yeast with juice that is at least room temperature or slightly warmer. Then, allow the yeast culture to begin to ferment over the next three to 12 hours. Once it shows signs of vigorous fermentation, add it to the bulk of your juice and let the process continue.

Besides dry yeast, there is also liquid yeast, which comes in two forms. The first is in what looks like a large test tube. You can shake it and dump it into your must. This is premade yeast culture, so it is already active and ready to go. You should refrigerate this until you are ready to pitch it, which slows down the yeast and keeps it fresh. Pitching is a term to describe adding yeast to the fruit juice or other plant extraction. You should allow liquid yeast to reach room temperature before you pitch it.

The other kind of liquid yeast is packaged in what I call a "punch pack." It looks like a foil juice pack, and inside you can feel a bubble move around. This is known as a yeast activator, and the yeast is in a free-moving plastic bubble. You must steady this bubble and smash it with the palm of your hand against a kitchen counter or tabletop. The bubble breaks, the yeast are released, and they activate. The liquid yeast costs about $5, and dry yeast only costs about $1. The only advantage of liquid yeast is that you get a rapid, strong fermentation. I have used both and can honestly say there is not much difference at the end of the day as far as the quality and taste of the wine.

CASE STUDY: SPOTLIGHT ON ALLISON OAKS VINEYARDS

Drew Renegar, General Manager
Pam and Gene Renegar, Proprietors
Allison Oaks Vineyards
221 East Main St.
Yadkinville, NC 27055
336-667-1388
www.allisonoaksvineyards.com

One of the most interesting small wineries in the North Carolina region is Allison Oaks Vineyards. Gene and Pam Renegar founded the winery, with their son Drew Renegar as the general manager. It began in 1997 when the family bought a grassy strip that was once an old airstrip, and the first vines were planted in 2000. They planted Syrah, Chardonnay, Viognier, Merlot, Zinfandel, Cabernet Franc, Cabernet Sauvignon, Barbera, Riesling, Nebbiolo, and Pinot Blanc. Gene grew up in a family that grew tobacco and raised poultry, while Pam's family was in dairy farming. Gene had farming skills and had made some attempts at creating homemade wine, but they wanted the winery to start off right. So they attended a local community college, where they completed a viniculture program and learned the art and skill of making wine.

The vines matured until 2004, when the family had their first harvest. They did not have enough of one type of grape to create a varietal wine, so they created two blends: Orchard White and Proprietor's Red. Since then, the Renegars have developed six additional varietal wines, including their signature Rose Zinfandel.

They use 100 percent of their own grapes in their wines but go to another local winery for a custom crush. They have a tasting room and banquet hall in downtown Yadkinville. They hold special events and rent out the banquet hall for weddings. Their hope is to create a restaurant that serves their estate wines. One of the family's favorite events is their "wine-rita" party: They blend margaritas made with their wine, serve food, and listen to a Jimmy Buffet-style band. They say it is one of the highlights of the year.

The Allison Oaks Vineyards has attracted the interest of the arts council and city council. They are central in a downtown revitalization project, and they support local artists by displaying and selling their art in their tasting room and at art gallery events.

CHAPTER 2

Basics of Winemaking

B efore you begin to make wine at home, first you must buy the right equipment. There is some investment that goes along with winemaking, usually between $80 and $120. The good news is that if you ever want to try your hand at making beer, you will already have the basic equipment to homebrew. You may wish to buy other equipment once you get the hang of your first few batches of wine, such as barrels, filtering systems, crushers, and destemmers, all of which will be explained in more detail later in this chapter. Once the winemaking bug bites you, there are many different upgrades that can make winemaking easier and faster to produce larger quantities.

In each of the recipes in this book, you will notice one of the ingredients listed is "making equipment." Let us begin with the pieces of equipment that are absolutely necessary in order to make the most basic wine. You could get away with using a trashcan, a hose, and empty soda bottles, but the likelihood of your wine turning out poorly increases dramatically. *In Appendix D, you will find a list of different resources where you can find winemaking supplies.*

STANDARD WINEMAKING EQUIPMENT

- Primary fermentation vessel
- Secondary fermentation vessel (carboy)
- Sanitizer
- Bottles
- Corks
- Corker

Primary fermentation vessel

The wine must needs somewhere to sit and ferment. There are two types for the fermentation process: open and closed fermentation. I would recommend the closed fermentation system because there is less chance of contamination.

Originally, wine was created in pottery vessels. Over time, Italians began using glass vessels called demijohns. These were placed in large baskets so they could be transported before wine bottles were used. In order to keep the wine fresh, they would put a layer of olive oil over the wine. The wine was served from these vessels, and the oil floated on top and created a barrier that kept the wine from turning into vinegar. The oil did not alter the taste of the wine much because it never could really mix with it.

If you have ever looked at a bottle of salad vinaigrette, you can see that the oil and vinegar are separated, and you must shake the bottle hard before pouring the contents on a salad. When the bottle stands still again, the oil will separate to the top.

Vessels for open fermentation

An open fermentation system means the vessel where the wine must is fermenting is not sealed. You can use a large plastic or glass container and create wine this way. Some of my first wines were created this way, and I had some marginal success. I had a large plastic bucket and covered it with a trash bag. The bag was not used to seal it, but it did keep bugs out. It was a rather weak grape wine, and I was determined to make much better wine, thus moved over to a closed fermentation system.

I bought a fermentation bucket that looked like a large pickle barrel with a wire handle. This is what most primary fermentation vessels look like. The main criterion of a plastic wine vessel is that it must be made of food-grade plastic, which means that it is safe to eat and drink from. These can be purchased from a hardware store, a winemaking supply store, a restaurant supply store, or online. Do not use a bucket that has been used for any other purpose. If there were any chemicals stored in the bucket, they can leach into your wine.

You may want to buy a bucket with a hole drilled near the bottom. The hole allows you to screw on a plastic spigot so the wine can be easily moved from one vessel to another. Most of the fermentation buckets you purchase at winemaking supply stores already have the hole. You will need a spigot to attach to the bucket, and it should cost less than $5. A spigot is a tap with a valve that allows you to drain the wine from the fermentation vessel. It is usually placed at the bottom of the bucket. The hole called the *bunghole* is usually a half-inch or more from the bottom of the vessel. This allows you to drain the wine and leave the lees behind. If you buy a bucket from a hardware store, you will have to drill the hole yourself and measure it so the spigot will fit.

Bacteria, fruit flies, and other nasty bugs love open fermentation, which is why I do not recommend it. However, it is a perfectly viable option for fruits that have a larger population of natural yeasts on their surface. Natural yeasts quickly make the juice inhospitable to other, less desirable microorganisms. That is not to say nothing can go wrong: If you notice a slimy, oily slick across your wine must, it is time to dump your wine. This is what is called the "mother," and is acetic acid bacteria, which is what creates vinegar. The more time your wine is exposed to the air, the more likely it will taste better on a salad than in a wine glass. Oxidation is another potential problem with open vessel fermentation. When your wine becomes oxidized, it will lose its color, turn brown, and spoil.

TIP
Some fermenters have marks on them to indicate 1-, 5-, and 6-gallon levels. If yours does not, fill the bucket with water at the different levels and mark these delineations both on the inside and outside of the bucket with a permanent marker.

Glass carboys are large bottles with a small opening that are used in wine fermentation. They are not recommended for open fermentation systems, as the top opening is not wide enough to allow healthy yeast to find its way to your wine.

Vessels for closed fermentation

In order to create a closed fermentation, you will need to add a lid to your fermentation vessel. Most plastic fermentation vessels have lids that pop on top and have a rubber gasket to create an airtight seal. When you purchase a fermentation bucket from a supply store, the lid is usually included. The fermenters are usually 7.5- to 12-gallon containers. If you wish to produce 5-gallon batches of wine, there should be a little space for the foaming that usually occurs at the beginning of fermentation.

Look on top of the lid to make sure you find another small hole — this is where the gas will escape. If you have ever cooked with a pressure cooker, you have seen the small release valve on the top. Carbon dioxide gas is released during fermentation, and without the hole, you will create a gas bomb. Eventually, the pressure will pop the lid off and make a mess. If the lid does not have a hole, many supply stores will drill the hole for you. In this hole, there is a rubber ring that creates a seal for the inserted fermentation lock. The fermentation lock is another small item that you will need to purchase. It is relatively cheap, but serves a very important purpose: It allows gas to escape but keeps oxygen and other unwanted visitors from finding their way into your fermentation vessel. One end has a small pipe that fits into the top hole in the fermenter lid. On top is a place to put sterilized water. Alternatively, you may wish to use a 3 percent solution of sulfite in the lock, which will kill any would-be invaders.

When your wine is fermenting, you will see bubbles created from the carbon dioxide in your fermentation lock. It will provide you with important information: when fermentation begins and ends. You should change the water in your fermentation lock every couple of days. Make sure it is sanitized or distilled water. If you use the sulfite in the lock, there is no need to change the solution.

 Reduce the number of times you open the lid of your fermenter. Each time you do, there is a risk of contamination.

Do not forget to place your fermentation lock on your fermenter. Imagine shaking a bottle of cola; when you open the lid, the liquid comes showering out. This same thing will happen if you forget to put on your fermentation lock.

An alternative to a fermentation lock is a tube placed in the drilled stopper. Insert the other end of the tube in a large glass or bowl of water. This is useful if your wine must is heavily fermenting and foam needs to be released early on in the fermentation process.

Carboy

There is another kind of fermenter that is often used, called a carboy. This is a large, glass bottle with a small neck. Though they can come in many different sizes, the usual size used for 5-gallon batches are 6-gallon carboys. Unlike the primary fermenter, you do not want too much headspace in a carboy. If you want to make a 1-gallon batch, you should use a glass jug or 1-gallon carboy. Be careful not to buy a 6.5-gallon carboy, as this may be too large if you plan to make wine from a wine kit. Too much headspace can lead to spoilage and oxidation of your wine.

Carboys work much the same as a plastic bucket, except you will insert a rubber stopper, or "bung," instead of a lid with a hole in it. These bungs are drilled with a hole, so a fermentation lock can be placed into the top.

As previously mentioned, secondary fermentation occurs after the primary fermentation ceases. Once the rapid bubbling and frothing has stopped, the wine is usually transferred to the carboy and racked off its lees. At this point, depending on the grape variety you are using, you may choose to initiate secondary fermentation, often referred to as malolactic fermentation. Malolactic fermentation occurs when bacteria feed on the malic acid in the wine and turn it into lactic acid. This is a natural process, although you can add bacteria to trigger it if you choose.

This process reduces the acidity of the wine and softens its sharpness. It mellows the wine and removes certain undesirable flavor components. However, not all grape varietals benefit from this. Crisper, fruity whites and lighter reds tend to go flat, as the natural acidity of the grapes is desirable in these varieties.

If you are making wine on a budget, you can get away with just one vessel, skipping the racking step and doing only a primary fermentation, or you can use two buckets instead of a carboy if you choose to rack your wine. Wine will mellow over six months to a year in the bottle, but it takes longer, and you risk having a lot of sediment in the bottles. These leftover lees can add unpleasant flavor, and things floating in the wine might turn off some people.

There is an advantage to using a carboy, and it has to do with the shape of the container. When aging wine, you want to reduce the amount of oxygen that comes in contact with your wine. Oxygen is bad for wine because it oxidizes it, and can change the color and flavor of your finished product. Bad bacteria love oxygen and can also spoil your wine in an oxygen-rich environment. Because a carboy is cone-shaped at the top, it reduces the headspace. Headspace is the area between the top of your wine and the top of the vessel. One of the gasses released from wine is nitrogen, which preserves wine and prevents spoilage. When you seal your carboy, the nitrogen will naturally form a barrier and therefore buffer your wine. It has less area to occupy in a carboy. The tighter you seal your carboy, the better your wine will be, because you contain the nitrogen and prevent oxygen from coming into contact with your wine.

Another way to reduce headspace is to add additional wine or juice to your wine, depending on where you are in the process of fermentation. Evaporation occurs naturally, and you will lose a little bit of your wine when you rack it off the lees. The less headspace you leave, the better chance you have of a perfect wine. It is suggested that when you are making more than a few gallons of wine, you should plan to make a little extra for use in topping off your vessel after racking off the lees.

There are carboys of all sizes to choose from, as well as demijohns, which are one size bigger. In this book, I include two recipes that use a 6-gallon carboy or a 1- to 1.5-gallon carboy. The smaller carboy is essentially a small glass jug. The standard equipment includes the 5-gallon carboy, and I will state whether you need a 1-gallon carboy.

If you are making 1-gallon recipes, I would recommend buying two 1-gallon carboys and using them instead of a plastic bucket.

The buckets are designed to hold about 6 gallons of wine; a 1-gallon recipe in a bucket this size will leave too much headspace. You can use one jug for primary fermentation and the other for secondary fermentation. The reason some of the recipes are for 1 gallon is merely for economic reasons. It takes a lot of fruit to make 1 gallon of wine, so a 1-gallon recipe is more affordable to create than a 5-gallon recipe.

When shopping for a bung to go into your carboy, you must make sure it is the right size, and that it has a hole drilled into it. Most home-winemaking supply stores can help you with this. You will use the same fermentation lock that you would use with the bucket type of fermenter.

TIP
Be careful when lifting your carboy. They are glass and they do not have a handle. A full carboy of wine can weigh close to 50 pounds. You should get someone to help you lift your fermenter. There will be times when you will need to lift it off the ground to a greater height. When you are racking off wine into another fermenter, a siphon will only work if the carboy you are racking from is higher than the carboy the clear wine is being siphoned into. You can buy a carboy handle that attaches to your carboy for around $5, and this will make lifting a lot easier.

Your fermenters are your most essential implements, though there are a few other standard items I would recommend in order to make the best wine possible. You could get away with not having these items, but you increase the risk of a bad batch of wine.

TIP If you are having problems with your significant other not agreeing with your winemaking, the best thing to do is to include him or her in the process of making the wine. It should be fun, and you will be glad you have an extra set of hands to help you out.

Fermentation lock and bung

In a closed fermentation system, you must allow the carbon dioxide that is escaping from the wine to be released from the fermenter — or the pressure will make the vessel burst. This is why an airlock is necessary. If you have ever seen or used a pressure cooker, there is a device on top that allows the steam to be released. An airlock and bung system does much the same thing.

It is important that unwanted bacteria and other microbes do not make contact with your wine, so it is essential to create a way for carbon dioxide to escape, while at the same not allowing bad microbes to get in. The fermentation locks also prevent oxygen from getting to your wine, as this can oxidize and spoil your wine. There are a number of different shapes of fermentation locks, but they all do essentially the same thing. You can fill the fermentation lock with a bit of sanitized water that should be changed daily during fermentation. Alternatively, you can use a 3 percent solution of sulfite, which need not be changed. If you look closely, you will see a water fill line in your fermentation lock. Air can escape through the water or sulphite solution in the form of bubbles, but the liquid creates a barrier that prevents microbes from getting in. Some fermentation locks have an extra bell-like piece. This creates another barrier as it percolates during fermentation. Even in this type of fermentation lock, sanitized water or sulphite is added.

As mentioned earlier, there is a rubber ring in a drilled hole that the fermentation lock is held in. On a carboy, a bung is needed to place the fermentation lock into. Bungs come in different sizes according to the size of the carboy it is being placed in. Ask a salesperson at a winemaking supply store which size bung you will need for your particular carboy. Most 6-gallon carboys take a No. 6.5-sized bung.

Sanitizer

Repeat this mantra over and over: "Clean your parts before you start."

You must always clean and sanitize every piece of equipment, including your hands, before coming in contact with your wine. You must sanitize every time you move your wine from one vessel to another, and your bottles must be sanitized before you fill them.

The two types of sanitizers I recommend are B-Brite and C-Brite, which come in powdered form. Dissolve a small amount of the powder in water and use the water to clean everything you are working with, including your hands. You can never sanitize something too much. The sanitizing solution will kill any bacteria or microorganisms that could hurt your wine. The great thing about these products is you do not have to rinse the equipment after you sanitize; the sanitizer will not hurt you or the wine. These products have an iodine base, which give them killing power. However, if you are sensitive to iodine, you might want to consider some other product.

Some people suggest potassium metabisulfite as a sanitizer, but there are other products that are better used for this purpose. If you use sulfites to sanitize, you could run the risk of oversulfiting a wine. Sulfites occur naturally in wine in small levels, but using too much in the process can run the risk of a smell of rotten eggs being added to the wine.

Sulfites in your wine

Sulfites are sulfur ions that naturally occur in all wines. Sulfites are often added in the wine to stop the fermentation process and are also added to the wine as a preservative to stop it from spoiling or oxidizing. Many organic wines claim to be sulfite-free, but this may not totally be true. All wines naturally contain some sulfites. Red wines contain less sulfites than white and dessert wines.

After 1987, wine bottled in the United States with greater than 10 parts per million concentration of sulfites is required to be labeled with the notification "Contains Sulfites." In November 2005, the European Union passed a similar law. If you are making wines from other fruits and vegetables, you should be aware that dried fruits and some dried potato products also contain sulfites as a preservative. Fresh fruits and vegetables used to be treated with sulfites, but in 1986 the U.S. Food and Drug Administration banned its use on raw food.

Some people cannot drink wine because they are sensitive to sulfites, and using extra amounts of sulfite can cause an even greater reaction. Many people I have known with sulfite allergies have no problem drinking my wine because I do not use an excessive amount — usually only 1 to 2 Campden tablets per 5-gallon batch. This can shorten the shelf life of a wine, but I personally have never had a batch of wine long enough for it to go bad. The shelf life of a typical wine made at home is a year or less. Some wines can be aged beyond this, but care must be taken to store these wines in a temperature-controlled environment.

There is some controversy regarding whether to add sulfites for fermentation or after fermentation. Those who believe that sulfites should be added at the end, or "brownies," feel that the slight browning of the wine at the end of fermentation is worth it for the chance of more complex wine. The reason for the browning is that sulfites act as an antioxidant. By not sulfiting the wine until the end, you allow wild yeasts to thrive and add more complex flavors as they ferment alongside cultivated yeasts that are added to the wine. The slight browning can be removed through clarification at the end of the winemaking process. Varieties that may benefit from this approach would be heavier reds like Cabernet Sauvignon, or whites like Chardonnay.

"We need to add sulfites to our wine to give them a greater shelf life. Our wines have levels of between 25 to 50 parts per million. This may sound like a lot, but imagine placing a million cans of soup side by side; it would stretch for miles. Now consider even 200 hundred parts per million; that would only stretch a few yards. The federal government allows 350 parts per million total sulfites in wine. This is even imposed upon wines imported to the United States. You will find that wines that are shipped longer distances, like from Australia or South America, will have more added sulfites because it helps stabilize them more to ensure that they maintain their integrity during shipping."

— Steve Shepard, vintner and general manager; RayLen Vineyards & Winery

"We do not believe that it is necessary to add additional sulfites to a homemade wine, unless you plan to age it. Most of the time, people will drink homemade wine long before sulfiting would become an issue."

— Mike Walkup, co-owner;
Advantage Beer & Wine Supplies

The other advantage of waiting until the end of fermentation is the formation of acetaldehyde, which creates off-flavors and odors in wine. This chemical is naturally formed in the process of fermentation, but it is in higher concentrations when sulfites are added. Most of the time acetaldehyde is not noticeable in wine, but the chance of it causing problems is increased with the use of sulfites early on in the process.

The other group, or "greenies," believes that sulfites should be added at the beginning of fermentation. They believe wild yeast dies off naturally in low alcohol concentrations in fermenting wine and therefore do not benefit the overall taste of the final product. They believe sulfites are needed to kill off wild yeast and malolactic bacteria at the beginning of fermentation. This is preferred if the winemaker does not want his or her wine to undergo malolactic fermentation to smooth the taste of their wine. The greenies do not mind a little browning and believe that it is important to kill any bacteria or yeast that can lead to the spoilage of wine. They do not mind the chance of higher concentrations of acetaldehyde, as they do not believe that even the higher amounts are detectable in most wines. Some varietals that might benefit from this approach would be lighter, fruity, or more acidic wines like Sauvignon Blanc or Pinot Grigio.

If there are no sulfites in your wine, the risk of spoilage increases. This would mean you need to be careful when cleaning equipment, during the crushing and pressing of grapes, and throughout the process of fermentation. The sulfites should be used in cleaning all of the equipment, but unlike some other sanitizers, it will need to be rinsed. When adding sulfites to wine to stabilize and kill off wild yeasts or bacteria, you should add ¼ teaspoon of sulfite for every 5 gallons of wine, which equals about 50 parts per million.

One of the common forms of potassium metabisulfite is Campden tablets. These are compressed tablets that contain about 75 parts per million of sulfite and should be used at the rate of about one tablet per gallon. While these are conveniently packaged and pre-measured, they can be difficult to use. They must be completely crushed with a mortar and pestle into a powder before it is added to the wine, and sometimes it is hard to dissolve. You may also buy potassium metabisulfite in a powder form that you can measure out per teaspoon. The powder form is usually cheaper than Campden tablets.

A **mortar and pestle** is an implement that is used to crush or grind a substance. It was often used in pharmacies, and a picture of it can often be seen on an old-fashioned pharmacy sign. The mortar is a bowl made of wood, marble, stone, or clay, and the pestle is a club-shaped instrument that is used to grind the material. This is a handy tool to have with your winemaking tools because it can be used to grind herbs, Campden tablets, roots, and other materials. Make sure you thoroughly clean, sanitize, and dry both the mortar and pestle between uses.

The potency of potassium metabisulfite decreases over time. It should be stored in a sealed container, and sulfite that is more than a year old should be used for cleaning purposes only, rather than being added to wine, because it is not as potent.

I would also warn against using chlorine products such as bleach, as this will leave an aftertaste in your wine. If you do choose to use chlorine, use it in diluted amounts, such as 1 teaspoon per 1 gallon of water. Never use soap to clean your equipment. Your wine will taste soapy because it will leave a residue on your equipment. Use the hottest water you can stand. You can even fill your dishwasher with your equipment, and instead of washing powder, you can use sanitizer. This also works well for sterilizing bottles before filling them.

If you have a question about whether to sanitize something, then err on the side of caution. I cannot tell you how many batches I spoiled when I first began making my own wine, simply because it became contaminated. It will not make you sick if you drink wine with traces of it, and more than likely you will smell a bad odor long before the wine hits your lips. If you ever get vinegar bacteria in your wine, the bacteria can linger in microscopic cracks and crevices. You will continue to ruin batches, and it is not worth the hassle of pouring what could have been a perfectly good wine down the drain because it turned to vinegar. In the long run, if you ever have a batch of wine turn into vinegar, buy a new plastic fermenter and recycle your old one.

You should only use your winemaking equipment for making wine. Do not use it for anything else. You should always clean and sanitize your equipment before you store it, and try to store it dry. When you use stored equipment, you will need to sanitize it again.

Bottles

You could leave the wine in a fermenter and drink it directly from there, but you would need to drink it quickly. As the headspace grows, your wine will spoil. It would be tough to pour it from a carboy, but you could rack it back into the primary fermentation bucket and dispense it from the bottom.

> **TIP** If you dispense your wine from the primary fermenter, do not forget to take off the fermentation lock. When the wine begins to pour, it creates a vacuum in the fermenter and will pull stale water from your fermentation lock into your wine. This is especially true if you choose to use sulphite solution in your lock.

I would recommend that you only store wine in 750-ml. bottles. Bottles last longer, are easy to store, and can be kept cool, which reduces spoilage. Keeping bottles in a cool place also reduces the chance of re-fermentation and popping bottles. In winemaking, bottles can be the most expensive thing you will ever have to buy. You can buy them from winemaking supply stores or directly from manufacturers. They are expensive to purchase online because of shipping costs.

I tell my friends that I will replace their empties with full bottles. When choosing a bottle, you should use ones that do not have a screw top and that are colored, not clear. Clear glass bottles can lead to changes in the wine when light strikes it, such as a faded color or a metallic taste.

You will not be able to put a cork in a screw top bottle, so you should not save any of these types of bottles. They do not work in a corker, so just recycle them. You will need standard-sized bottles of 750 ml., as these are the easiest to work with.

Wine bottles come in all different colors, so you can choose your favorite to keep or give as special gifts once you have filled them. Wine bottles come in all shapes and sizes. The shape and size do not matter much — with one exception. If you are making a sparkling or champagne-type wine, you will want to purchase champagne bottles. They are made with thicker glass because the contents will be under pressure. If you use a champagne bottle, you will also need champagne stoppers and wire. If you use a regular bottle when the contents are under pressure, the bottle can explode, and a cork can be easily pushed out.

Ask your friends and family to save wine bottles for you. You might want to think of a place to store them because pretty soon you may be overrun with them.

> **TIP** For every gallon of wine, you will need five 750-ml. bottles. 750-ml. bottles are the standard-size wine bottle. For a 5-gallon batch, you will need between 23 to 25 bottles.

If you are still having difficulty locating bottles after you have asked friends and family members, then you can ask the owners at a local bar, pub, or restaurant for their empty bottles of wine. Most of them just recycle their bottles at the end of the night, so tell them to hold the bottles and the boxes they are packaged in, and you will pick them up. You can pick through them and recycle the bottles you do not need or cannot use. You are doing the world a favor by recycling.

There are two different types of winemakers: Those who care about labels stuck on used wine bottles and those who do not. I will be honest; I started off the first type and, over time, became the second. Below are some of the tricks I learned to remove bottle labels:

1. Use heat and water. Steaming the labels or pouring hot water over them will loosen most labels, but not all. The glue used on labels today is tough because wine should last for decades, and the label must last that long as well. The hotter the water, the easier it will be to get the label off.

2. Try dry heat. You can use a hair dryer to heat the label and try to peel it off that way. This does not work as well as using water and heat.

3. Use ice. When a bottle of wine is placed in a wine bucket, the label will slip right off. You can try to put your bottles in a cooler with ice and water.

4. Try abrasive cleaner or steel wool. Rinse the bottle well after using these methods. This method can usually get off a tough label when combined with heat and water.

5. Soak the bottle in water with a little added ammonia or dish soap.

6. Try soaking the bottles in wallpaper remover. Be sure to rinse the bottles well before using them.

7. If you really want a clean bottle, you may need to use a razor to scratch it off. Be very careful.

Some Web sites suggest using gasoline as a solvent. Never do this. Gasoline is dangerous and has no business in home winemaking. For the same reason, do not use any commercial sticker remover, as these often contain petrochemicals.

You can cover up old labels with new labels if you do not want to take the time to try to scrape them off. Scraping off wine labels is a lot of work, and I eventually gave up. I would rather drink the wine rather than make sure the bottle looks perfect. I did make a mistake in my relinquishment: I did not bother to label the bottles in any discernible way. This became a problem because when I made more than one batch of wine, I forgot which bottle contained a particular wine. Mark the top of your corks — just remember what your scrawl means six months later. A master list or spreadsheet can be a handy way to remember what kind of wine is in which bottles, or you can consider special bottle types for each variety you wish to make. It is best to use some type of label, even if it is as simple as a peel-and-stick mailing label. It does not have to be fancy; it just has to say what it is in the bottle. *Chapter 11 further discusses making your own labels.*

Corks

If you have bottles, you must find a way to seal them; corks nicely do the job. They expand when in a bottle and seal the wine from the outside world and any bacteria that could spoil your wine. The bad news is corks are not reusable. Once they are removed, they need to be tossed, although you could mulch or recycle them as wood.

Corks come from an oak tree that grows in Southwest Europe and Northwest Africa. It is actually the thick bark that is harvested to use as corks, but it takes a tree nine to 12 years to grow to the right thickness. Once a tree is harvested, it takes another nine to 12 years before it can be harvested again. The average cork oak lives between 150 to 250 years. These trees are protected from being cut down in some countries like Portugal. Out of the bark that is harvested, 15 percent of each tree is used for wine corks.

Corks come in different sizes, just like bottles. Make sure you buy the right-sized corks for the bottles you are using, or they may not fit correctly. But corks come from a type of tree that is becoming endangered, so those who are eco-conscious should take note. The rate of use for these trees is greater than replanting rates. As a result, many wine companies have switched to using rubber synthetic corks. These are a fine choice, and I have not noticed a difference in the taste or color of wine that has a synthetic cork. For those purists who believe corks allow wines to breathe, synthetic corks are a poor choice. If you use natural corks, keep in mind they can often be recycled into other products, like cork flooring or bulletin board material. Many recycling centers accept them. But both natural and synthetic corks have their advantages and drawbacks.

Cork preferences of wineries and vineyards:

"We use synthetic corks for most of our wines, except our high-end reserve wines, in which we use real corks."

— Mark Terry, general manager and winemaker;
   Westbend Vineyards

• • • • • • • • • • •

"Urraca only uses real corks, which are traditional in winemaking."

— John Langley, owner; Urraca Wines

• • • • • • • • • • •

"We use natural corks on some of our wines, and we did use synthetic for a time on the others. We have replaced the synthetic corks with screw caps; in fact, five of our 15 wines have a screw cap. The screw cap allows the wine to age in a more even and consistent fashion. When you use natural cork, you might open a case with wine that uses corks and find a couple perfect bottles, some that are flat, some that still has a harsh flavor, and some that still need to be aged longer. This does not happen with screw caps. Some of the synthetic corks are made from chemicals like plastic and do not allow the wine to breathe properly."

— Steve Shepard, vintner and general manager;
   RayLen Vineyards & Winery

• • • • • • • • • • •

"We recommend Nomacorcs as the best brand of synthetic corks. It can fit into most floor and bench corkers."

— Mike Walkup, co-owner;
   Advantage Beer & Wine Supplies

• • • • • • • • • • •

"We use some synthetic corks, but the wines do not age as well, so we use natural corks with our red wines. Screw caps are the best way to preserve any food or liquid, but the equipment needed to put them on wine bottles is cost-prohibitive to smaller winemakers."

— Mike Helton, vintner; Hanover Park Vineyard

There is a danger in using natural corks: cork taint. It is caused by a chemical called TCA (2,4,6-trichloroanisole), which is created by fungus that lives in cork fiber. It ruins the taste of a wine, should you use infected corks. Soak corks in sanitizer before you cork the bottle with them. This also creates a better seal on the bottle. Do not soak them too long (less than ten minutes works best) because the cork can swell and make it harder to insert into the bottle. Make sure the corks you are trying to use are long, straight corks. Do not use tapered corks.

There are different grades of cork. The higher the grade, the more expensive the corks are. Synthetic corks are cheaper than natural cork. Cheaper natural corks are a composite "pressed" or aggregated cork, which means they are pressed together with added glue. These are not the best choice if you plan to age a wine.

Corker

You could try all day, but you will never be able to push a cork all the way into a bottle by hand — eventually, you will need a corker. The most basic and least expensive corker is a hand corker. It takes some hand strength because you need to compress the cork by squeezing it together before pushing it in with a plunger. Hand corkers work best with cheaper compressed corks. They do not work too well with natural or synthetic corks because they are too hard to compress. You are better off using a floor corker, described in the next section.

Be sure the corks are inserted all the way into the bottle. This is where friends and family can help. You need someone with upper arm strength to do it, and it helps to at least have someone to hold the bottle. It is best to have the bottle on the ground rather than on a tabletop to prevent it from slipping.

This ends the list of essentials. The next two sections discuss upgrades and other extra implements that will make your winemaking world a happy and harmonious place. Most of the items in this first section can be bought together as a winemaking kit from a home-winemaking supplier. You can often buy a kit for less than what it would cost to buy the pieces individually, or about $80. You might also consider buying a wine concentrate kit to try out first. These kits come with all of the ingredients to make 5 gallons of wine. Everything is measured out and included. However, the instructions are usually very rudimentary and sometimes hard to understand. The instructions provided in this book will help you make a great wine.

INTERMEDIATE SUPPLIES

You can immediately upgrade some of your equipment. These are not serious upgrades, like the list in the advanced section; rather, they are small items that can allow you to control the results of your winemaking and make some of the actions much easier. These are not usually included in beginner home-winemaker kits, unless you are lucky.

Intermediate supplies:

- Bottle brushes
- Bottle filler
- Hydrometer or refractometer
- Floating thermometer
- Wine spoon

- Tubing
- Clarifier/stabilizer
- Acids
- Other additives

Bottle brushes

In order to clean bottles and carboys, you can buy bottle brushes. Both bottles and carboys can have sediment form on the bottom and can be hard to shake loose with just simple rinsing. Bottle brushes come in different sizes. You can buy the smaller one for your bottles and the long, large ones for your carboy. Bend the handle slightly on the long brush before inserting into your carboy so you can reach all the nooks and crannies. The bend is especially helpful in cleaning the upper part of the carboy. Use the bottle brush on the bottles, especially if they are used bottles, before you sanitize them. Get hot water and fill the wine bottle, then use the brush to clean the bottle of any sediment. Hold the bottle up to a bright light so you are sure you cleaned everything. Leaving sediment is asking for trouble later on.

After using your carboy in fermentation, fill the carboy about a quarter-full of hot water, and use the brush to clean the bottom and the sides. Without a brush, this is almost impossible unless you fill the carboy with hot water and let it soak an hour or more. Even then you will have difficulty.

Do not use your brush on a plastic primary fermenter. Brushes can cause scratches in the plastic, which is a great place for microorganisms to hide. In fact, you should never use any kind of abrasive brush on a plastic fermenter.

Bottle filler

A bottle filler, in some ways, belongs in the essentials list. You can get by without having one, but once you have one, you will wonder why you did not buy it earlier. When filling bottles from a fermenter, you must manually cut off the flow. The bottle filler fits on the end of the tubing, which you can read about below. It is a long, plastic pipe that fits into the wine bottle. At the end of the pipe, there is a spring mechanism. When you push the pipe down, it allows the wine to flow. When you release the pressure, the flow stops. I would still recommend that you place something on the floor, like an old towel, beneath your wine bottles, as you will have some spillage.

From past experience, I would recommend you wear special winemaking clothes. Wine stains and juice is sticky. One time, I was wearing a relatively new pair of leather shoes while making mead, and somehow honey dripped on the top of these shoes. The shoes were ruined and my wife was not happy. Every time she saw me getting ready to make wine or mead, she told me to put on my honey shoes. These shoes became the official winemaking loafers.

The other function of the bottle filler is to create headspace. Up until now, I have said headspace is bad, but for bottles, a little headspace is necessary. Look at any commercial wine: You will see a space between the top of the liquid and the cork. This is to allow some off-gassing of the wine. Wine will release some gasses while it is in the bottle. If you do not allow some room, then the gases will make room by pushing your cork right out of the bottle — it will sound like a pop gun. The bottle filler takes up some room in the bottle when it is inserted. Even if you fill the bottle to the top with wine, when you remove the filler, there will be some space left in the bottle. It is the perfect amount of headspace. You do not want to recreate Old Faithful. It is better to drink wine than to try to figure how to get it off the ceiling. Bottle fillers usually cost less than $20. It might be a good idea to buy one early in order to save time, mess, and aggravation.

Hydrometer

At the beginning of all of the recipes, you will see the letters OG and FG. OG stands for original gravity, and FG represents final gravity. These letters are followed by a number and are important because they lead to the ABV, or alcohol by volume. Remember that yeast eats sugar and converts it into alcohol. The amount of fermentable sugar in a wine will determine how much alcohol a certain wine should contain when it has finished fermenting. Another abbreviation you will see is SG or specific gravity. This is the same measurement as OG and FG.

This is important to know for a couple of reasons. First, when you are fixing your wine at the beginning and preparing it for fermentation, knowing the OG will help you determine if you need any more sugar or if the mixture needs a little dilution. Knowing the final gravity will help you determine when fermentation is over. If the wine has not quite reached the final gravity, it could mean that your fermentation is stuck, that you picked the wrong kind of yeast, or that it is still quietly fermenting. Bottling the wine too soon could mean it may be too sweet; might not have enough alcohol for taste; or could could continue to ferment in the bottle.

In order to understand specific gravity, think in terms of density. You can try the following experiment to understand how this works:

1. Fill a wine bottle to the top with water.

2. Place an unsharpened pencil, eraser side down, into the water. It will float.

3. Mark on the pencil where the top of the bottle is.

4. Empty the water into a container and add a cup of sugar to it. Mix it well until the sugar dissolves.

5. Fill the bottle with the sugar water.

6. Place the pencil, eraser-side-down, into the liquid. You will notice the line you marked on the pencil the first time is higher above the water line. This is because the mixture of water and sugar is denser than just plain water.

The pencil you used in the experiment is a crude but effective hydrometer. Wine hydrometers are sealed glass tubes with a paper label inside them. The bottom usually contains mercury or some other heavy metal to weigh it down, just like the eraser. There are usually three different scales, but the one that shows specific gravity is the one that has 1.000 on it and numbers above and below 1.000. This number 1.000 is the specific gravity of plain water. The numbers below the 1.000 are higher, and this is because liquids that show this reading are denser than water. The numbers above the 1.000 on the scale, like 0.999, are less dense than water. Alcohol is less dense than water. You could repeat the pencil experiment and pour rubbing alcohol into the bottle; the pencil will sink lower than the line for plain water.

On many hydrometers, there are two other scales. The first scale is the Balling Scale, or "Brix." The Brix scale shows you how much sugar there is in a liquid. The other scale is simply called "potential alcohol content," which measures the highest amount of alcohol you will be able to achieve with specific amounts of yeast and fruit. You can conduct a reading of the potential alcohol before it ferments and then after it is finished. Subtract these two numbers. All three of these scales use the same process of determining what the specific gravity of a liquid is, but each scale is just another way of reading it. It is similar to a thermometer that has Fahrenheit and Celsius scales. These are both measurements of the same level of mercury.

This works because the sugar was converted to alcohol, and the amount of change in gravity is alcohol replacing the sugar. This potential alcohol is the same as the ABV number on the recipe. The Balling reading shows how much sugar is in the mixture. It is assumed your must is denser because of the amount of sugar in it. When you are finished making the wine, your balling will be lower.

You really just need to concentrate on the specific gravity. If you want to try to figure out what the alcohol content will be before you make a wine, and you only have OG and FG, you can use this formula:

$$\text{Approximate alcohol content (\%)} = \frac{OG - FG}{0.0074}$$

I have made it easy for you and already calculated the ABV in each recipe. It is important to know the potential alcohol content of a wine because it will help you decide which yeast to use.

If your wine has a potential alcohol content of 18 percent, but you are using yeast that dies out at 14 percent, then you will end up with a sweet wine with less alcohol. You may desire less alcohol in your wine, but alcohol does significantly contribute to the overall taste of a wine. Having too much or too little alcohol can make a wine weak or overpowering.

Be aware that temperature can alter a hydrometer reading. Try to read a hydrometer at room temperature. If it is too cool or hot, your reading can be off because liquid contracts when it gets hot and becomes denser when it cools. The following is an adjustment scale:

°F Adjust
40 - .002
50 - .001
60
70 + .001
80 + .002
90 + .004
100 + .005
110 + .007
120 + .008
130 + .010
140 + .013
150 + .015

You should also purchase a hydrometer-testing jar. This makes it easier to read and uses only a small amount of wine. You should always clean your equipment after use, but never return a wine sample back into the fermenter. You can taste it if you like and dump the rest when you are done. I have found that tasting the wine during the different stages of fermentation has helped me learn what it should taste and smell like. This helps me determine when a wine is done or when there is a problem that needs to be fixed.

Refractometer

A Brix refractometer is an alternative to a hydrometer; it is somewhat more expensive but more convenient to use. A precision optical instrument, refractometers are designed to measure the concentration of solids in solution. It does this by measuring the refractive index — the speed at which light travels through a liquid. The denser a liquid, the slower light travels through it, and the higher its reading will be on the refractometer. Most winemaking and brew shops carry these, and they are also available online for somewhat less money. Be sure to purchase one that can read up to 32 percent sugar.

The hand-held refractometer is simple and easy to use, requiring just a drop or two of your liquid to be placed on the built-in prism. The cover is placed over the prism, and the device is held up to the light for viewing through an eyepiece somewhat like a microscope's. The display is like a standard, old-fashioned thermometer. A dark line will appear somewhere on the scale visible through the eyepiece and will correspond to the percentage of sugar in your juice. To convert this percentage to the maximum percentage of alcohol your juice can produce, simply multiply by 0.55. This is the same technique professional wine makers and growers use to determine the right time to pick the grapes. A grape picked at 25 Brix (25 percent sugar) will yield a wine of approximately 13.75% ABV. A quick way to do a rough estimate of potential alcohol is to divide the Brix reading by 2 and add 1.

25 x 0.55 = 13.75% ABV

As discussed above, the percentage of sugar in your juice or other fermentation liquid will determine the amount of alcohol in your wine. Knowing this percentage is important so you know how much sugar you have, which determines how much yeast you will need and what the finished ABV will be. Much like a set of measuring cups for a cook, the right equipment will make it much easier to tell how much of your various ingredients you will need to use.

> **TIP** When testing to see if a wine has stopped fermenting, you should not just rely on one reading. Test it over a couple of days; if the reading remains constant, then it has stopped. If it is still changing, you should wait until it has completely stopped fermenting before you consider bottling the wine.

Floating thermometer

The temperature of your wine is very important for fermentation and aging. If your wine is too hot or too cold, the yeast will die off or go into a suspended state. If you kill the yeast, you will have to start all over again. When aging a wine, you want it cool so things can settle down and refermentation does not reoccur. If you can dedicate a temperature-controlled room for winemaking, this would be ideal. Most people must use their kitchen, bathroom, garage, or an outbuilding for their hobby. These areas are a little harder to control the temperature in.

Before pitching the yeast into a wine must, you must make sure it is as close to room temperature as possible, or maybe a little above. Do not pitch the yeast above 75 degrees Fahrenheit. If you can keep the must at about 68 degrees Fahrenheit during primary fermentation, this is a good temperature for healthy yeast growth. If you drop below 60 degrees, your yeast will go dormant.

I have found that floating thermometers work the best for testing wine. You can place them in the fermenter to take a direct reading. The other time to check the temperature is before taking a hydrometer reading for as accurate a reading as possible.

The fact that the thermometer floats makes it easy to read and retrieve. I recommend tying a monofilament string on the top loop so your hand does not go anywhere near the must. Remember to sanitize the thermometer every time you use it.

If your must is not the right temperature, here are some suggestions to get it there:

- Buy a brew belt or a FermWrap heater. The wrap goes around the bottom of the carboy like insulation and is temperature-controlled. It is water-resistant and fits snuggly. The FermWrap will work on a plastic bucket or a carboy. A brew belt should not be used on a glass carboy. They are less than $30 and plug into the wall. They look like you would expect — a belt that wraps around the fermenter.

- Wrap the fermenter in a blanket. Do not use an electric blanket because it is not safe.

- Wrap insulation around your fermenter. It will keep the must at a constant temperature; however, it gets ruined if it gets wet.

- Wrap it in foam rubber. This works similar to insulation, but it can get wet and be washed.

- If it is too hot, place the fermenter in an ice bath. This will cool it quickly. It should not be used during rapid fermentation.

- Place in a basement or spring house. These places are cool and have a constant temperature. These are also good places for aging your wine.

- Place a wet T-shirt over your fermenter and place a fan next to it. This is a homemade air-conditioning system. This will cool it quickly, but it is not recommended during fermentation.

- If you have to heat a liquid, such as water to dissolve honey in mead, you can use what is called a wort chiller. This is usually used for brewing beer, but will work with a wine or mead as well. It is copper tubing that is inserted into the liquid, and cold water runs through it. The heat from the liquid is transferred out of the liquid with the flowing water. This is a quick way to drop the temperature in order to get it close to the temperature needed to pitch the yeast.

Wine spoon

As previously mentioned, you should have equipment that is used for winemaking and no other tasks. You do not want to use the same spoon that you used to stir last night's chili. You can purchase a wine spoon that has a long handle, which is usually made from plastic or stainless steel. You should not use a wooden spoon because bacteria can hide in the pores, no matter how much you clean it. Of the two options, the stainless steel is better because the plastic spoon can get scratches that can hide bacteria. You can purchase one from a winemaking supplier. They are usually long enough to stir must in a fermenter and are easy to clean and sterilize. The spoon will be useful for the following activities:

- Stir in yeast when you pitch it into the must

- Stir and mix wine ingredients

- If you need to heat any ingredients on the stove, you will need to stir so it does not burn

- Stir a must to aerate it for yeast to begin fermenting

- Stir and dissolve sugar or honey in a must

- Remove fruit, cheesecloth, or bag from the fermentation vessel

Tubing

There are numerous beginning winemaking kits that include tubing. You will find that it is almost essential in transferring wine to another vessel and is needed for transferring wine into bottles. This is one item you can buy from a hardware store or an aquarium supply store. Measure the diameter of your spigot and bottle filler before you purchase it. Also, make sure that it is food-grade, flexible tubing. It is relatively cheap, so buy it by the yard. However, it is difficult to clean, so if there is any buildup, you should recycle it and cut a new piece of tubing.

Before cutting, measure how much you will need to go from the fermenter to a bottle or another fermenter. Once you cut it, you cannot tape it back together, so take the time to measure it first. You can have a couple of different sets of tubing for different tasks. Before using the tubing, fill a container with sanitizer and soak the tubing, then run hot water through it. After using it, repeat this process and make sure there is not water in the tube. Hang it up to dry.

Clarifiers/Finings

As a wine ferments, it produces dead yeast cells and loose protein molecules. These particles can affect the clarity of wine, and this can be seen when looking at a wine in a wine glass with a light behind it. To what degree they can affect the wine depends on the grapes, the yeast, and any other additives. These clarifiers bind to these particles and settle them at the bottom of the fermenter.

Finings are much like a clarifier, but finings not only clarify a wine and make it sparkle, but they also help with problems of color, taste, and bouquet. It is recommended that some sort of fining should be used in all wines, but here are some of the main reasons that a fining can be used:

- It removes bitter and harsh flavors in a wine.

- It reduces the amount of unpleasant aromas.

- Oxidation can occur in a wine and add a brown pigmentation to a wine. Certain finings help avoid this oxidation process, which prevents the stripping of color.

- Even after a wine has finished fermenting, it may still be unstable. In order to prevent refermentation, finings — specifically, stabilizers — help keep this process from occurring.

- Dead yeast cells can be suspended in a wine during fermentation; finings — specifically, clarifiers — help make these cells drop to the bottom of the fermenter, and the clarified wine can be racked off the top.

- There are other protein particles that can be suspended in wine, and clarifiers can also bind with these charged particles to help remove them from your wine.

- It is not only the flavor and bouquet of wine that people enjoy; it is also the luster and color. Finings help polish a wine and make it sparkle in light to give it a brilliant, bright appearance.

There is not just one fining that will work for every wine, and there is no one fining that can do everything in a particular wine. It takes knowledge and a little experimentation to decide what fining is right for your particular wine. Sometimes it takes combinations of finings to cover all the desired effects.

Some first-time home winemakers may feel a little intimidated using finings. If you are using a wine kit, the necessary finings are usually included in premeasured quantities. There are usually instructions included that tell you when to add these finings during the winemaking process. If you are using concentrated juices that have already been processed, then you will likely not need finings.

If, on the other hand you are attempting to create wine from grapes, fruit, or even vegetables, you may have a greater need to use finings and clarifiers. There is a greater chance you will need to know what each of the finings are, how they are used, and at what measurements they should be added to your wine. Many of the finings have directions on how to use them, but when you buy in bulk or transfer the finings to another container, you can use the measurements that are listed below.

With some finings, such as in the case of clarifiers, you can see the results; your wine is more clear and polished in appearance. Sometimes finings can alter the taste and smell of a wine, so the results are not visible. Finings work in two different ways. In some cases, they attract particles through electric charges. If you want to see a simple demonstration of how this works, then try this: Pour a little black pepper on a sheet of paper, then take a comb and run it through your hair. Place the comb near the pepper; you will see the pepper move and become attached to your comb. This is because you created a charge in the comb by running it through your hair. That static electric charge then pulls the pepper that has a different type of electric charge. Certain finings work on the same principle; the finings replace the comb, and instead of pepper, there are charge protein particles. Once these two things bind together, they become heavy and sink to the bottom of the fermenter.

The second type of fining reaction is absorption. These types of finings are like a sponge soaking up water, as they draw in particles and then sink to the bottom of the fermenter.

For the beginning winemaker, there may be some confusion about when to actually add finings to a wine. There are three main times when you will add finings:

1. Before fermentation:

There are times when you will add finings to a wine must before fermentation, such as if you want to kill off any wild yeast with sulfites before you add any cultivated yeasts. Wild yeasts and bacteria can alter a wine's taste or even spoil a wine. If you are using fruits high in pectin, you may want to add pectic enzyme in order to prevent a pectin haze later on in the fermentation process.

2. After fermentation:

The most common time a fining agent is added is right after the fermentation has ended. Adding them during the fermentation process could kill off or stop the yeast from fermenting the grape juice. If you accidentally add a fining too soon, you could try to make a yeast starter and start the fermentation, although this may not always work. In some cases, you might have to settle for a sweet wine or pour it out and start over again.

Making a yeast starter:

1. Siphon a cup of unfermented juice into a sterile glass cup.

2. Add yeast and stir gently.

3. Cover loosely with a paper towel and secure with a rubber band around the rim of the glass. Allow the starter to stay at least 70° F for six to 12 hours.

4. Add starter to the wine must and stir gently.

When using finings at the end of fermentation, you will be speeding the process of dead yeast cells from falling out of the wine and creating the gross lees in the bottom of the vessel. This will reduce hazes that can form from suspended particles.

3. At the time of bottling:

Before you bottle the wine, you may decide the wine needs a little work. You may decide to add finings in order to adjust the clarity or color of wine; in some cases, you can make minor adjustments to bouquet and flavor. It may seem that this part of the process is during the same period of time mentioned above. However, if you want to have the yeast drop out of the wine, you would do this immediately after fermentation and then rack the wine again before bottling it. During the period of time mentioned here, you would be adding the fining just prior to bottling; you may not necessarily rack the wine again before you add it to the bottles. If you intend to age your wine, there is a period of time between the cessation of fermentation and bottling. You may decide to add finings before aging, or wait until you are actually ready to bottle your wine.

Some professional winemakers use filtering to "polish" their wines:

"We do our wine in small batches. We clarify them and then filter them before bottling them."

> — Drew Renegar, general manager;
> Allison Oaks Vineyards

• • • • • • • • • •

"Our wines need to be flawless; therefore, we filter all of our wine. We also cold-stabilize and heat-stabilize our wines. This process allows the consumer to drink a wine today or put it on the shelf to age a year or two."

> — Steve Shepard, vintner and general manager;
> RayLen Vineyards & Winery

• • • • • • • • • •

"We do not filter our red wines — we rack them until they are clear. I have found that barrels act as filters and have found that many wines seem to clear after being in a barrel for even a short time. We do filter our white wines, but we do not barrel age them except one barrel-aged Chardonnay. To me, homemade wines all have a slight taste to them that filtering can successfully remove. I spent money buying a small pump-and-filter combination, but it was one of the greatest investments I made, and [I] encourage all home winemakers to filter their wine."

> — Mike Helton, vintner; Hanover Park Vineyard

And some don't:

Many high-end wines in California are un-fined. Professional winemakers tend to feel that fining may remove some of the desirable complexities that enable their wines to stand the test of time. Wines that age well over longer time periods generally do better when less is done to them. Wines intended for more immediate (within two years) consumption are more frequently filtered or fined.

You may use finings in combinations. One fining can clump the particles together, while another fining or topping agent can be added to the wine to speed up the process of those clumps falling to the bottom of the fermenter. Clarifiers are types of finings that specifically help clear your wine. When you look into a glass of good wine, it is clear without any sediment. This is because it has been removed, and clarifiers do this by chemically binding themselves to proteins, then sinking to the bottom of the fermenter. The clear wine is then racked off into a carboy or fermenter before it is bottled. This process is done after the wine has finished fermenting, although in some recipes and wine kits, Bentonite clay is added early on. Some winemakers also filter their wine after clarifying it, before the wine is bottled. This removes any particles that could not be removed with a clarifier. You should have some of these on hand. The following is a list of some clarifiers:

- **Bentonite:** This is a type of clay that absorbs large amounts of protein particles from an aqueous solution. It is gray in color and is mixed directly into the wine until it is dissolved. To clarify a 5-gallon batch of wine, add 2 tablespoons of bentonite to ½ cup of hot water. Stir the mixture well until it is completely dissolved. It will look like gray water and should then be added to the wine. Stir the mixture in until it mixes throughout the wine. Cat litter does have Bentonite in it, but it is not recommended you use it for this purpose, as it may contain other toxic chemicals. Bentonite used for the purpose of wine clarifying can be purchased at a winemaking supplier, or you may also find it at health stores as an internal cleanser of the body.

- **Sparkolloid:** This is a combination of diatomaceous earth and a blend of polysaccharides. This creates a positive charge to the mixture that will then neutralize negatively charged particles in your wine, which will then sink to the bottom and form lees. It does not strip your wine of color or flavor, so it is a preferred type of clarifier. For a 5-gallon batch, you can use 5 teaspoons or 1 teaspoon per gallon. It will usually only remove protein molecules, which leads to what is called protein haze.

- **Isinglass:** This is a gelatin-like substance found in the swim bladders of fish, especially Beluga Sturgeon. It is a completely clear substance that grabs onto yeast and then pulls it to the bottom of the fermenter. This is used at the end of fermentation. It is used in clearing beers such as Guinness, thus some vegetarians will not drink beers and wine that use isinglass as a clarifying agent. You can make your wines sparkle using 1 ounce of isinglass per 5 gallons of wine.

- **Kieselsol/Chitosan (Kitosol 40):** These fining agents create a negative charge, which attracts protein particles for removal from the wine. These products do not usually leave any aftertaste, odor, or off color, so they are safe to use. Kieselsol is colloidal silica, which is a solution of silicon dioxide suspended in water. Kieselsol is often used in conjunction with gelatin. It was originally created to replace tannin.

- **Pectic enzyme:** This breaks down pectin in fruit and is very important when creating a non-grape wine. It can also increase the yield of white wine grapes. It can be used with red wine grapes as it aids in the disintegration of the grape during primary fermentation. It also breaks down the cellular structure in fruit and allows for more juice extraction. Pectin can create a haze that can be seen while looking at wine in a glass. It is usually added at the beginning of the winemaking process. It usually comes in a powder form. You can add ¼ teaspoon directly to the juice or extract about a ½ cup of juice and mix it before adding it. Make sure you stir it well, as the powder can clump. Store pectic enzyme carefully, as it lasts longer when refrigerated, but it should be discarded after two years. It should be noted that pectic enzyme will be ineffective if it is added at the same time as bentonite clay.

- **Gelatin:** This is the material used to create gelatinous food items, although it is not recommended that you add these sweetened or flavored gelatinous foods to your wine. You can use plain, unflavored gelatin from the grocery store, or you can use gelatin purchased from a winemaking supply store that is formulated specifically for winemaking. The latter is more expensive. Either will work well with red wines to clear particles that can make them cloudy, as well as to reduce unwanted or harsh flavors in a wine that can occur when a wine red wine is young and has not aged. If you decide to use gelatin in a white wine, you should use wine tannin as a topping agent to speed up the settling of particles. You should also consider using bentonite about one to two hours after using gelatin in your wine to absorb any excess. When used as a fining, you should add about a ⅛ of a teaspoon for every 1 gallon of wine. You might want to consider mixing it in a ½ cup of hot water before adding to the wine must so it is properly dissolved. You can add the ½ cup of hot water to the gelatin slowly while stirring the mixture. Once it is dissolved, pour into the wine quickly and mix it before it cools, or it may gel and be useless. Two days after adding the gelatin to the wine, you should rack it to a sanitized container.

- **Irish moss:** This is not the same as moss found on trees. It is actually a species of red algae that is also called carrageen moss. It attracts other proteins and solids, and drops to the bottom of the fermenter. It is used in a popular drink in the Caribbean called Jamaican Irish moss, which is a combination of Irish moss, flavoring, and sweetened condensed milk. Because it is an emulsifier, it turns into a gelatin-like solid when boiled and is used in lunch meats and ice cream. You should add about 1 teaspoon in a 5-gallon batch to clarify it.

STABILIZERS

Stabilizers stop the fermentation process and prevent the growth of other microorganisms. Some common stabilizers include:

- **Potassium metabisulfite powder** and **Campden tablets** have already been mentioned as good products to kill off wild yeasts and bacteria that may spoil wine.

- **Potassium sorbate** works a little differently in that it will not stop the fermentation process; rather, it will stop the refermentation of a wine in a bottle. This can occur if the yeast still present in the wine begins to digest residual sugars. Potassium sorbate can add a geranium-like odor to a wine (especially if it is added during malolactic fermentation) that people may not like. It is only necessary to consider using potassium sorbate with wines that have 3 percent or more residual sugar. Before bottling, add ¾ grams of potassium sorbate per 1 gallon of wine, or 200 parts per million, and add potassium metabisulfite.

Acids

You can purchase acids separately as citric, ascorbic, malic, and tartaric acid. I would recommend an acid blend instead. A blend consists of 67 percent tartaric acid and 33 percent malic acid. There are chemicals that reduce the level of acid in a wine, such as calcium carbonate and potassium bicarbonate. Each of these costs a few dollars. Before adding these to a wine, I recommend you buy a pH- and acid-testing kit. You can read about these later in this section.

Other additives

You can add yet more chemicals to your wine. You might consider adding a water conditioner if you have hard water such as gypsum or Burton salts. These additives condition the water without hurting the flavor of your wine. In order to help your yeast out, you can add yeast nutrient and yeast energizer. Each of these can help a stuck or slow fermentation, and each of these additives costs only a few dollars. Before adding any of these, consider whether you really need to, as some of them have the potential to add odd flavors.

Some wine kits contain powdered oak that is added to a wine at the beginning. This brings out flavors such as smoky, wood, and vanilla in your wine. The powder will settle out, but the flavor will remain. This is added instead of aging your homemade wine in an oak barrel. Some kits contain oak chips that are added after the wine has finished fermenting. This will leave a woodier flavor to the wine, and the wine will be racked off these chips before bottling. Both the powder and chips are often made from used wine barrels.

> **TIP** I have found that an egg white works well as a clarifier in a pinch. You can add two egg whites to a 5-gallon batch. Make sure you only use the egg white, by separating the yolk from the white. Most grocery stores carry containers of egg white; in that case, use 2 tablespoons of egg whites.

ADVANCED SUPPLIES

Are you ready to upgrade? Are you a "gear" junkie like me? In this section, I will offer you a list of equipment that is either an upgrade of your current equipment or additional equipment that can help you in your quest to make even better wine.

The following is a list of upgrades and wine gear you might want to add to your home winery.

Floor/Bench corker

Is your hand and back tired yet from forcing corks into bottles? There is an easier way. A bench and a floor corker work the same as a hand-held corker. One can sit on your counter; the other is tall and can be used on the floor. Many of these come from Italy and have a durable design, so you will never have to replace them. You can cork up to about 150 bottles an hour. These use a lock-and-load method: Drop a cork in the top and put the bottle snuggly underneath, then pull down the arm, and the bottle is perfectly corked without any damage. Sometimes you can end up butchering corks using a hand unit. If you want to use synthetic corks, or you want to create many 5-gallon batches, then this is well worth the investment. These units sell for around $100.

Larger fermenters

You can buy larger carboys and demijohns, up to 15-gallon sizes. These are heavy and are not very portable or practical. I would recommend considering other types of primary fermenters. Some fermenters come with screw-on plastic lids; if you have ever had to get a lid off a primary fermenter, you will know that this can be difficult. These buckets have the spigot and airlock.

Stainless-steel fermenters can run a few hundred dollars and can hold up to 30 gallons of wine. It has an inflatable gasket that allows you to brew any amount of wine because it allows you to adjust the level of the lid. These units run about $500 and are not generally very mobile. Other than these options, you can use a larger plastic fermenter. This is more like the stainless-steel fermenters that you find in wineries, only smaller. They have many extras added on and, like the stainless-steel varieties, can hold large volumes of wine.

Pail-opening tool

This can make getting the lid off a plastic fermenter much easier. It is a metal hand tool that can get up and under the lid and save your fingers from getting hurt trying to pry off the lid. This life-saving device goes for about $5. It is in the advanced list because it is not a necessity; however, I have one and cannot live without it.

Filtration system

There are different levels of filtering, from the reasonable to the extremely expensive. The cheapest way to filter your wine is to use coffee filters in a funnel. Filtering is not a necessity for most amateur home winemakers. It is more of a matter of aesthetics, if you do not want sediment in the bottom of the bottle once a wine has settled.

There are a number of clarifiers mentioned in the last section. If you are patient, most wine will eventually clear. If you do want a filtering system, expect to pay between $50 and $500. The lower end of a filter system is a gravity-fed kind that uses disposable filters. This works great for 1-gallon batches, but it gets clogged for anything larger than that, and you end up using multiple filters for one batch.

The next step up is a pressure system you can hand pump. This works better than the gravity-fed and can clear much larger batches up to 10 gallons. This costs about $100.

You then get into the much more expensive jet models. These have electric pumps that force the wine through a number of filters. This will produce very clear wine, but for me, it is just not worth the expense.

Crusher/Destemmer

You can buy crushers that are not destemmers. A destemmer is mostly for those who want to create grape wines. Fruit crushers can be hand-cranked or motorized. They are very similar to a wood chipper in that it grinds the fruit with rotating teeth. This prepares the fruit to be pressed. These range from $200 to $400. A destemmer can run about $500.

Wine press

The most common fruit presses are the ratchet-and-screw types. They have a plate that moves down on the fruit when you pump the ratchet or turn the screw wheel. Some presses have a bladder that gently crushes the fruit without extracting bitter flavors and tannins from the seeds.

You can buy a small tabletop press for 1 to 5 gallons of wine for about $130, and the other larger screw-and-ratchet models run upward of $500. A bladder press can run into the thousands of dollars.

Bottle washer

This is a piece of equipment that can screw onto your faucet to allow you to clean your bottles and carboy. A bit like a spray nozzle for your garden hose, it puts the water under pressure to clean better and has a push trigger that only releases water when you press your bottle or carboy onto it.

Bottle tree

This is a quick way to sanitize and store bottles. It is a tower that you place your bottle on branches that stick out. This keeps the bottle upside down to dry and stay cleaner. Some models have an attachment that will spray sanitizer up into the bottles before you hang them.

"We barrel-age all of our red wines, and we also do a barrel-aged Chardonnay. We use many older used barrels. These work great and impart just enough oaky flavors without being harsh. We use French and Hungarian oak barrels. We age our red wines for about three to five years. There is a lot of evaporation that occurs, but to me this is like the reduction of a sauce. The flavors become more complex and concentrated. There are changes that will occur while a wine is in a barrel that just will not occur if you do not age it."

— Mike Helton, vintner; Hanover Park Vineyard

Barrels

There are three main types of oak barrels you can buy to age your wine: American, Hungarian, and French. They come in different sizes, but they can be expensive. Be careful: Used barrels can leak. If you purchase a new oak barrel, you will be asked what level of toasting you want. This is similar to roasting coffee. The inside of the barrel is toasted to different levels of char. This imparts different amounts of oak flavor to your wine. Oak barrels range from $200 to more than $500 per barrel for smaller barrels, and into the thousands of dollars for larger French barrels. They do not last forever and can wear out and leak. An average barrel will last about three to four batches.

One thing to note is that if you age a white wine in a barrel, then you can use that barrel for white or red wines in future batches. However, once a barrel has been used for a red wine, it can only be used for a red wine, because a white will take on a red color. The first time a barrel is used, it will impart the strongest oak flavor, so you may want to create a wine that usually has a strong, oaky character, like a Chardonnay.

There are alternatives, such as liquid oak and oak chips, that can be added to the wine. The oak chips soak in an aging wine and then are removed. The chips often come from used barrels that have been broken down. This imparts a decent oak flavoring without the oak barrel price.

Juicers/Pitters

These tools are great for making wines with fruit ingredients other than grapes. A steam juicer uses hot water to extract juice from fruit. This makes extraction easy without the need to crush and press. A steam juicer costs about $200. A pitter is great for getting pits out of cherries or similar fruit and can cost about $40.

Transfer pumps

These pump wine from one vessel to another quickly. These are electrical units that can pump 1 to 3 gallons a minute and come with a price tag of about $200.

Siphon

These are a much cheaper alternative to a pump. A wine siphon is a long tube within a tube that, when depressed, starts wine moving from one vessel to another. These cost less than $20, and I cannot live without mine. The alternative is sucking the wine through the tube to start the wine flowing, but this is not the most sanitary way to move wine.

Funnels/strainers

Funnels come in all shapes and sizes. Some have strainers that will fit inside. They can catch large particles as wine passes through.

It is a nice alternative to filtering, and can catch pulp and pits from fruit. These cost less than $10, including the filter screen that is washable and reusable.

Pulp bags

If you are tired of trying to use cheesecloth to place fruit in when making wine, you can buy a nylon bag to put your fruit pulp in. They are convenient because they are washable and reusable. They cost less than $20 and come in different sizes. Cheesecloth can also be used for this purpose, but I have found you must dispose of them after one use.

Upgraded faucets

You can change the faucet on your fermenters to a high-flow lever faucet. You may even consider an in-line faucet. This can be placed between two pieces of tubing and gives you control over the flow. Each of these only costs a few dollars.

Collapsible jug

This is just what it sounds like: plastic jugs that can be folded up when you are finished with them. They are great for home winemakers who have limited room to do their hobby and need to save on storage space. This is the type of fermenter I started with, and they work fine. They cost about $10 — great for the home winemaker on a budget.

Sulphite tester/pH testing kit

There are a number of test kits for your inner chemist. These use different solutions and papers to test the amount of acid or the amount of sulfite in your wine. There are kits to test levels of malic acid, residual sugar, and lactic acid. I love to fool around with these kits, but if you follow the recipes closely, you will not really need to use them. Your taste buds and nose are your best testers. Drink what you like and dump the rest.

CASE STUDY: SPOTLIGHT ON WESTBEND VINEYARDS

Mark Terry, Winemaker and
General Manager
Westbend Vineyards
5394 Williams Road
Lewisville, NC 27023
866-901-5023
www.westbendvineyards.com

The Westbend Vineyards is spread over 60 acres of prime vinifera vineyards on the edge of the Yadkin Valley. They take their name from the Yadkin River, which lies to the west of the vineyard.

The owners planted their first vines in 1972, even though other farmers in the area said it could not work. Jack Kroustalis, one of the original owners, refused to be daunted by the naysayers. The original vines were placed in the rolling terrain and grew well in the dense clay they were planted in. Today, there are vines of Chardonnay, Cabernet Sauvignon, Riesling, Merlot, and Sauvignon Blanc grapes that are growing strong along the banks of the Yadkin River.

Westbend produces about 8,500 cases of wine, spanning 20 different varieties. *Wine Spectator* magazine has scored Westbend wines the highest of any North Carolina wines.

CHAPTER 3

Making Wine from a Kit

"Good wine is a good familiar creature if it be well used."
— William Shakespeare (1564-1616); *Othello, II. iii* (315)

Before you jump into making wine from grapes, it is recommended that you try making wine from a kit. These can vary in price and difficulty of use. Much of the difference has to do with the quality of the grape juice used. When pressing grapes, the first press is the premium juice to be used as a wine. It has the most complex taste and ages well. It improves over time and is full-bodied. There are times, especially in the creation of red wine, when a wine is pressed twice: Once when they are first placed in the primary fermenter, then again once the wine has sat on the skins for a while.

Relax before you make the wine:

"Before starting to make wine from a kit, remember to relax. Read the instructions once, then sit down and have a glass of wine. Pick up the instructions and reread them a second and even a third time. The greatest errors in creating kit wines are not reading the instructions and dumping the ingredients in too soon. Once they are in the wine, they cannot be removed. In some instances, putting in additives or even flavoring juices can have disastrous effects."

— Mike Walkup, co-owner;
Advantage Beer & Wine Supplies

FIRST TIME USING A WINE KIT

Wine kits can be a great way to begin winemaking at home. They have everything in premeasured amounts and simple directions. However, that does not mean that you will not need a few skills to make a great wine the first time. Here are a couple of items you will need to do during the process of making wine from a kit or any other way.

1. **Sanitation:** You should get into the habit of sanitizing your equipment, your work space, and your hands. You can use the sanitizing powder and mix 1 gallon of sanitizer ahead of time or use liquid sanitizers according to the directions printed on the label. You must clean everything before starting. Even if you sanitized your equipment after you last used it, you will need to sanitize before you begin to make a new batch.

2. **Measuring specific gravity:** This is done using a hydrometer and a testing vessel. You will draw some of the wine using a wine thief or siphoning some off. A wine thief is a

long glass or plastic tube that can be inserted in the wine for a sample to be removed. Do not stick a cup into the wine if possible, and if you do, make sure the cup and your hand are sanitized. Add the wine to the testing vessel and drop the hydrometer into the vessel, or if using a refractometer, place two to three droplets of wine onto the prism. The hydrometer will float, but make sure there are no solids or bubbles floating in the wine must. If the hydrometer has more than one scale, make sure you are reading the specific gravity scale. You will notice a slight dip in the wine next to the hydrometer. This is caused by surface tension and is called the meniscus. Read the number at the bottom of this dip. Make sure you write this number down on the directions, so you will remember it later. After the initial hydrometer or refractometer reading, you may take a few more to determine when fermentation has ended or needs to end. Never return the sample to the wine. You may taste it or pour it out.

3. **Racking:** This is removing wine from the lees on the bottom, and is usually done using a siphon. You can buy a siphon or can try siphoning by mouth — although this latter technique can lead to contamination. In order for siphoning to work when transferring wine from a carboy into another vessel, you must place the container that you are siphoning from higher than the container you are siphoning into. Once the suction has started, it is important not to allow the suction to stop. This can happen if the bottom of the siphon hose is above the liquid at any time. The other issue to be careful with is not to stir up the lees during the racking process. Before the racking begins, the fermentation vessel should be placed in position

and left there for at least an hour before racking. This allows any dislodged sediment to settle back on the bottom of the fermenter. Hold the bottom of the siphon about an inch above the sediment and be careful not to stir it up. Near the end of the racking process, pull the end of the tubing out of the wine so it does not begin to siphon up any of the lees. You will lose a little wine in the racking process, but what you will be left with is clear wine.

If you are racking wine from a fermentation bucket to a carboy, the process is much simpler because you do not need to siphon the wine. You will still need to place the fermentation bucket higher than the carboy and allow it to settle before racking. The main difference is that tubing is attached to the spigot at the bottom of the fermentation vessel, and the liquid drains by gravity into the lower vessel. The hole in the bucket is high enough to allow the wine to rack off the lees and leave the lees behind. Do not tip the bucket during the racking process, or you could dislodge the lees and they will be transferred to the carboy.

Once you have finished racking the wine into a carboy or other vessel, including an aging barrel, it is a good idea to top off the wine. This decreases the headspace. Whenever possible, it pays to make a bit of extra wine specifically for topping off. You can also top it off with other similar wine from a previous batch or from a commercially purchased bottle. It is not a good idea to add juice back, as this may restart fermentation.

Making wine from a kit is very simple, but if you are like me, I often misplace the paper, or it gets wet and ruined while I am trying to make the wine. Most instruction kits follow the same basic structure, so you can use the following set of wine kit instructions as your basic guide.

> "One of things that I would recommend in order for someone to make a great wine is education and experience. In fact, experience is education. I continually go to seminars and seek out education about new technologies and methods of winemaking. I believe this is essential in making a great wine and continually improving the process."
>
> — Steve Shepard, vintner and winemaker;
>   RayLen Vineyards & Winery

WINE KIT INSTRUCTIONS

Primary fermentation

Days 1 through 5

1. Make sure all of your equipment is clean and sanitized.

2. You may have an additive pack that needs to be prepared, such as bentonite. Add the bentonite to a cup of hot water and mix it until the bentonite is thoroughly dissolved, then add it to the primary fermenter.

3. Open the main juice concentrate bag. Be aware that some kits have a second smaller bag of juice that is usually added at the end of the fermentation process to add flavors such as raspberry or peach. Do not open this bag until it is ready to be added to the wine. It may be tricky

to get the cap off the juice bag. They are not screw tops and usually have to be pried off. I suggest using the tine of a fork to pop the cap off. Be careful to do this over the fermentation bucket, or you may fling juice onto the floor. When you are done emptying the bag, add a little warm water, swish it around, and add it to the fermenter. The juice concentrate is high in sugar, sticky, and thick, so the water helps to dilute any residual juice.

4. Add any other additives such as oak powder to the must. Do not add finings or clarifiers at this stage; place them to the side. Bring the water up to the proper level (often 6 gallons) using room temperature water. Many kits are 6-gallon kits, but read the box to see how much wine the kit produces. Stir the mixture of water and juice well.

5. Use a wine thief, or use the spigot at the bottom of the fermentation bucket and fill the hydrometer-testing container. Take a hydrometer reading and make sure you record it.

> **TIP** Some fermentation buckets have gallons marked on them. For those who do not have a mark, add water using an old milk jug to the 5-gallon mark and then the 6-gallon mark. Mark each of these levels on the inside and outside of the fermentation vessel with a permanent marker.

6. Most of the time, wine kit wines have been balanced and adjusted; therefore, the hydrometer reading will be in the range of 1.080 and 1.090. A refractometer reading should generally be somewhere between 22 and 28 Brix. This

number will help you determine the potential alcohol content of your wine.

7. If you have a dry yeast packet, add it to ½ cup of warm water and stir to rehydrate. Add the yeast (called pitching the yeast) to the fermenter and stir.

8. Add the lid to the fermenter and insert the fermentation lock. Add the necessary amount of sanitized water or sulfite solution to the fermentation lock. Place the fermenter in a warm place for the next few days. It is crucial that the place is warm enough for the yeast to thrive, or else fermentation will slow or stop. If this happens, warm the fermenter with a FermWrap or warm blanket for a while until you see signs of life. You will know fermentation has begun by bubbling in the fermentation lock. Do not open the lid to check the wine, as this risks contamination or oxidation. In five days, check the hydrometer or refractometer reading and make sure that it is about 1.020 or around 3 Brix. This means that primary fermentation has ceased.

Secondary fermentation

Days 6 through 10

9. Rack the wine from the primary fermenter to a carboy. Be sure you remove the fermentation lock from the top of the primary fermenting vessel when you are racking because the process creates a vacuum within the fermenter as the wine is being transferred. If you leave the fermentation lock on the fermenter, you risk the water or sulfite solution being pulled into the wine. It will also

slow down the flow of wine into the secondary fermentation vessel. As you rack off the clear wine, you will leave the lees behind. Add the bung and fermentation lock to the carboy. Make sure you clean and sanitize the primary fermenter and store it upside down.

10. Allow the wine to finish primary fermentation, go through malolactic fermentation (if applicable to your verital), and begin to settle out. Toward the end of this period of time, you should check the hydrometer/refractometer readings more frequently to determine that secondary fermentation has ceased. You will know this when the readings stop changing and are around 0.995 or less, or 1.8 Brix. This is your final gravity, and you should write this number down. If you are using a hydrometer, you can now determine what your alcohol content is by subtracting the two numbers, such as:

1.080 - 0.995 = 0.085, or 8.5 percent alcohol

If using a refractometer, subtract your final Brix from your starting Brix and multiply by 0.55 to get your percent alcohol:

24.0 Brix - 1.8 Brix = 22.2 Brix x 0.55 = 12.21% alcohol

Fining and aging the wine

Days 17 through 22

11. Use your wine thief and remove some of the wine. Mix in your potassium sorbate and potassium metabisulfite with

the borrowed wine. Mix it well and return the sample back to the wine. Mix it well.

12. Use your wine thief and remove some more wine and add any other finings or clarifiers to your wine sample. Add the sample back to the wine and stir it well. If you have oak chips, you would add them at this stage. Replace the bung and fermentation lock.

 You can buy a wine thief from a winemaking supply store. For a cheaper version that works just as well, buy a cheap turkey baster.

13. For the next three days, vigorously stir the wine for 5 minutes, three times a day. Slightly tip the carboy and shake it back and forth. This dislodges any trapped gasses in the wine, unless the wine kit is for a sparkling wine. If you need to add a flavored juice, it is usually done during this stage.

14. Allow wine to sit in a cooler place the next two to three weeks. It will begin to settle out and may need to be racked one more time, depending on whether any sediment forms.

15. You may age the wine in the carboy for a few more months. This will smooth out the wine and give it more complexity and character.

16. When you are ready to bottle the wines, rack the wine into the primary fermenting bucket. Attach a hose and bottle filler, if you have one, to the spigot on the bottom.

Fill the bottles, but leave a little bit of space at the top. If you are using bottle filler, you will leave enough space because the filler displaces the room when it is filling the bottle. Once the bottle filler is removed, the right amount of space is left behind.

17. After the bottles are filled, you can use the corker of your choice to seal the wine. You can then age the wine in the bottle for up to a year. Many kit wines are meant to drink quickly after making it and are often the best to drink after about a month. If the wine has very little alcohol and is sweet, it is often made to be drunk quickly, as it does not age as well as higher alcohol wines.

18. Store the bottles in a cool, dry place. The more stable the temperature is, the longer the wine will stay fresh.

Wine kits can be a lot of fun to work with, and there are hundreds of different ones you can try, from Chardonnay that is pressed from grapes grown in France, to a kiwi strawberry Pinot Grigio that is a sweet, refreshing summer drink.

Following are some key tips to keep in mind to ensure that the wine you create with a wine kit turns out right every time.

"Never use any metal of any kind — in spoons, strainers, or containers. The metal can cause a reaction and give an off-taste to the wine. Stainless steel is OK, but I prefer the old-fashioned method."

— Richard Schlicht, home winemaker

TIPS

Tip No. 1: Follow the instructions

You have a general outline of how to make a kit wine above. Wine kits are not just randomly thrown together. Professional winemakers usually create them to ensure you will be successful in home winemaking. Many premium wine kits have multipage instructions with specific times to rack, add additives, and stir. You should look over these carefully. Even if you recently used the same wine kit, the instructions may have been changed slightly in order to improve the results, so it is worth reading over them again. There are reasons for these changes; for example, it may be that they are using a different yeast strain that could alter the amount of sediment it produces. They may also modify finings or other additives because a particular batch of juice included in the kit has differing requirements from a previous batch. Even experienced winemakers read the directions, so spend those few extra minutes reading — or you could ruin a wine with a simple mistake.

Tip No. 2: Start it right

Make sure that you are using the right amount of water when you start off your wine. The recipes mentioned in this book contain 5-gallon recipes, but as mentioned in the directions for using a wine kit above, most wine kits are for 6-gallon recipes. The exception is dessert wines, which are usually 3-gallon batches. It is very important to read the instructions and look at the box to determine how much wine the kit is supposed to produce. If you do not add enough water, you can end up with a harsh-tasting wine that may be high in alcohol and will not taste like the wine it is supposed to produce. If you add too much water, you will end up with a wine that is watery, weak, and low in alcohol level. On Day 1, make sure you double-check the instructions before you top off the water. Make sure you are using the right-sized fermenter for the particular wine you are making; it should not be too big or two small. You should choose an 8-gallon primary fermenter for a 6-gallon recipe and a 6-gallon carboy for secondary fermentation. Remember, you will lose a little wine in the racking process, but this is calculated in the wine kit recipe.

Tip No. 3: Record your process

In order to produce the best results with a wine kit, you need to document your process. It should include dates, times, temperatures, hydrometer readings, and other important information. You will be able to reproduce results when using a particular wine kit or even new ones. If the wine did not turn out the way you expected, you might find where you made an error and know how to fix a particular batch or prevent the same mistake in the future. *In Chapter 6, you will find a sample page for a wine journal.*

Tip No. 4: Maintain a level of patience

One of the common mistakes of first-time winemakers is being too impatient. They want to drink it too soon, before it has properly aged. When they taste the wine when it is too young, it may have harsh flavors, which may lead the new winemaker to believe that he or she did something wrong. Time will smooth out these flavors — patience is the cure.

The other mistake is when a new winemaker opens up the primary fermenter to see how his or her wine is progressing. Every time the lid is opened, the wine is exposed to oxygen and microbes. But once the process has begun, there is no reason to check the wine several times. It must be allowed to ferment and go through its natural process. The bubbling that occurs in the fermentation lock is how to determine when fermentation has begun and when it has begun to slow down; there is no necessity to open the lid to view the fermentation process. You can get samples from the spigot for hydrometer/refractometer readings. You can use a wine thief to sample wine from a carboy. If you need to check the temperature of a wine, you may have to open the fermenter, but this should be done quickly with a sanitized floating thermometer. If you have a stuck fermentation, you may have to make the decision to check the temperature.

Tip No. 5: Cleaning and sanitation

When you have finished with a piece of equipment, or you are preparing it to be used in the winemaking process, you must make sure that it is clean and sanitized. Being clean means that you have washed it with hot water and a clean rag to remove any debris. This is just part of the process. After it is clean, then it needs to be sanitized. Each piece of equipment needs to be immediately cleaned and sanitized after use and stored in a clean area. It is a good idea to seal smaller items in a zip-top bag for storage to reduce the opportunities for contamination. When you are ready to use it, you must clean and sanitize it again. The hottest water you can use without burning yourself should be used to clean the materials. Remember: Do not use any detergents, as these can leave a soapy residue. Once you are sure it is clean, then sanitize it. It is during the period between uses that bacteria and other microbes have time to grow, so do not assume that because you cleaned it well after using it, it is still clean and sanitary.

Tip No. 6: Stir well

The juice used in kits is thick and viscous. It must be stirred vigorously in order to mix the water and the juice on Day 1. If not, the thick juice will lie on the bottom of the fermenter, and the water will be floating on top of it. This will create errors in your sugar readings. If the yeast is pitched under these conditions, they may not reach the juice or be overworked — which can lead to a stuck fermentation. If the yeast reaches the juice, it may not be able to survive in the high-sugar environment. So when the yeast is pitched, it should be gently and thoroughly mixed.

When additives are added to the wine, it must be vigorously mixed so the additives are evenly dispersed and dissolved in the wine. This is also the reason that finings such as Bentonite are prepared before they are added to the wine, or it can clump and lie uselessly on the bottom.

After fermentation, it is very important to stir the wine hard enough to create slight foam. Continue to stir until the foam disappears. During fermentation, CO_2 is created and dissolved in the wine. CO_2 can bind with finings and prevent them from settling at the bottom of the fermenter. Stirring the wine vigorously releases this CO_2.

If you do not want to open a fermenter to stir it, you may also rock it back and forth to mix the contents. Be aware that stirring or rocking will dislodge any sediment on the bottom, and it could take a few days for it to settle again.

Tip No. 7: Control the temperature

Temperature is important for yeast to begin and continue fermentation. If it is too hot or cold, or even if the temperature fluctuates a lot, the yeast can slow down or die. The typical temperature range for fermentation is 68 to 78 degrees F, or 18 to 24 degrees C. Kit wines do well within this range because it creates a balance between fermentation and the production of esters, which are flavor compounds created with the production of alcohol. It is the alcohol taste we perceive.

In commercial wineries, white wines are often produced in temperatures below 55 degrees F. They can create wines over a longer period of time and allow for a slower fermentation. They have greater control of the timing of producing a wine and being able to keep a stable temperature.

Once you have created wine from kits a couple of times, the next logical step before jumping to crushing and pressing grapes is creating wines from grape juice.

CASE STUDY: SPOTLIGHT ON
RAYLEN VINEYARDS & WINERY

Steve Shepard, General Manager
RayLen Vineyards & Winery
3577 Highway 158
Mocksville, NC 27028
(336) 998-3100
www.raylenvineyards.com

In 1998, Joe and Joyce Neely purchased land in the Yadkin Valley of North Carolina. In 2000, the first grapes vines were planted. In the fall of 2001, RayLen opened their tasting room. During the first year, they bought some of the grapes from other local vineyards to augment their first vintage. They chose their varietals based on what others were growing in the area. There are now 35,000 European varietal grape vines growing on the property.

Their general manager and vintner, Steve Shepard, has an extensive history and education in winemaking. Shepard has been making wine commercially since 1980. In 1989, Shepard began making wines at the first Yadkin Valley winery. As RayLen was being built, Shepard had a hand in the design, which included planting ten different European varietals. This was a winning choice because within the first three vintages, RayLen Vineyards & Winery was awarded more than 200 medals at various statewide, regional, and international competitions.

Robert Parker, a famous wine critic and writer, has recognized Shepard for his 1991 vintage wines, and RayLen has been proclaimed one of the premier wineries in *Wine Spectator* magazine.

CHAPTER 4

Wine From Juice

"Wine is one of the most civilized things in the world, and one of the most natural things of the world that has been brought to the greatest perfection, and it offers a greater range for enjoyment and appreciation than possibly any other purely sensory thing."

— Ernest Hemingway

Experts on wine kits:

"The biggest difference of making a wine from grapes as opposed to a kit is that you will need a little more patience in creating the wine; you will need a larger fermentation vessel to accommodate the grapes, a fruit press, and an acid titration kit."

— Mike Walkup;
Advantage Beer & Wine Supplies

. . . .

"One of the best ways to learn to make wine is to volunteer at local wineries. You can start by helping picking grapes at harvest time. You can also help them with bottling and labeling. These are great times to ask questions and learn more about the process of winemaking from professionals. When you decide to try your hand at make wine from grapes, you will already have a source of grapes and even equipment if you need it. I sell off extra juice to people to make wine at home at cost."

— Mike Helton, vintner; Hanover Park Vineyard

The juice that comes with kits is already balanced and ready to use with the additives, either already added or are included in the kit. Making wine from fresh juices is slightly different in that they have not been prepared and do not have premeasured additives. You can buy grape juice for making wine from a winemaker supply store. They usually do not come with instructions, so you must follow a recipe to guide you. In the latter part of this chapter, there are recipes for creating a red or white wine using grapes. Other than the crushing and pressing that is involved, the process is the same.

You can make award-winning wine using grape juice rather than crushing them yourself. In fact, many large commercial wineries, like the Biltmore Estates, buy already-pressed juice from other vineyards when using varietals that they are not growing on the estate. Sometimes it is easier to transport juice then trying to transport tons of grapes, especially if they are coming from a distance.

If you want to try your hand at making a wine from juice, you can try the simple recipe below. It will not necessarily make award-winning wine, but it will make a nice, sweet wine that you can easily share with friends and family. Most brands of frozen grape juice are made from Concord grapes. They are sweet and have a memorable taste. These are the types of grapes that are used in most grape jelly. This wine is not meant to be aged; rather, it should be drunk quickly. It is slightly sweet and is great as a summer sipping wine and can be added to tonic water to create a wine spritzer.

USING JUICE IN WINE RECIPES

Frozen Tundra Wine

Yield 1 gallon/3.8 L
OG = 1.09 FG = 1.014 ABV = 10%
Brix: 20 / 1.83 = 11% ABV

Ingredients:

24 oz. frozen grape juice concentrate
(should be 100 percent juice, with no added sugar)
3 cups granulated sugar
1 packet dry wine yeast
1 gallon water
Bottles (3 to 5 bottles)
Corks
Corker
Siphon hose
Bottle filler
Primary fermentation bucket
1-gallon glass jug (carboy)

Instructions:

1. Defrost grape juice concentrate to room temperature. Add concentrate and water to carboy. Stir vigorously and dissolve sugar into the mixture. Add lid to fermenter and attach fermentation lock. Let sit for 24 hours.

2. On Day 2, pitch the yeast and gently stir. Attach fermentation lock and seal the fermenter. Allow to ferment for three weeks.

3. Rack clear wine into carboy off the sediment. Allow the wine to sit for another week and settle.

4. Rack into fermentation bucket. Attach tubing and bottle filler. Fill the bottles of wine and cork immediately.

5. This wine does not age well, so drink it within the first couple of months.

You can try this same simple recipe with any frozen juice concentrate, as long as it is 100 percent juice with no added sugar.

Once you have tried the Frozen Tundra recipe, you are ready to make wines from juices and juice concentrates on your own.

FRESH JUICE

You can ask at a local winery or vineyard if they are willing to sell you some pressed juice, or you may go online to find a source for fresh juice. Look around late summer/early fall during harvest time to find fresh grape juice. If you live in an area that produces wine, visit nearby vineyards and wineries to see if you can purchase fresh juice or grapes. Also, it may be possible to obtain second crop grapes for a reduced price. Second crop grapes are smaller clusters that form after the first flush of spring growth and pollination of the primary bunches. Because they form later, they will have a lower sugar level, and many vineyards do not include them in their harvest. If left to hang for a few days or a week or two longer, they can make a very cost-effective alternative to first crop juice.

You can also locate growers online using various help-wanted advertisements, such as Craigslist. Occasionally, growers will let you have grapes or juice free of charge if you agree to pick them yourself.

If you buy the fresh juice, it will not have any preservatives and will have a short shelf life. You will need to be prepared to begin making the wine immediately to prevent any spoilage.

STERILE JUICE

Sterile juice usually has potassium metabisulfite added to it to kill off any wild yeast and prevent spoilage. If you are lucky, the pH, acid level, and sugar may have already been adjusted. You will be able to use this juice much the same way you did in a wine kit. Both fresh and sterile juice comes in 6-gallon pails, so no water is needed unless you need to dilute it after testing for sugar and acid content.

JUICE CONCENTRATE

You can purchase juice concentrate in a can. This is much the same as the juice included in wine kits. It has a longer shelf life and has preservatives added, and it has most likely been balanced for sugar and acid. Read the instructions on the can to see how many cans you need to buy to make a 5- or 6-gallon batch. Usually, you will need at least two cans. Make sure you sterilize the can's top before using. You can buy juice concentrates from winemaking supply stores. If you are using fresh — or even sterilized — juice, you must learn how to test for the sugar content, acidity, and pH of your juice before fermenting your wine. In wine kits, this has already been done for you.

SUGAR

"In Wisconsin, we don't have as much sun [a much shorter growing season than California], so I use sugar to fortify my wine. I boil all the water to purify it. Then I boil the water and sugar together. I add acid [lemon juice], which inverts the sugar, which makes it good for fermenting."

— Richard Schlicht, home winemaker

If you look at wines on the shelf of your favorite wine shop, you would find that most food-friendly red wines are in the range of 12% and 12.5% ABV (alcohol by volume), and a typical dry white is about 11% to 11.5% ABV.

You should aim for these numbers when making wine at home if you plan to serve your wines with food. This means for a typical dry red wine of 12% ABV, you must start with 22 degrees Brix. The Brix scale is usually one of the scales on a hydrometer or, alternatively, can be measured with a refractometer. This measures the amount of sugar in a wine must.

A 22-degree Brix wine must is a measure of the approximate amount of sugar in the juice. A way to understand this number is if you had 100 grams of grape juice, and it contained about 1 gram of sugar, the must would be considered to have a 1-degree

Brix. So if you have a 22-degree Brix wine must, this means that the mixture is about 22 percent sugar.

The yeast will then ferment this sugar at about a rate of conversion of 55 percent ethyl alcohol, and the rest is converted to 45 percent carbon dioxide. When looking at a Brix number, the way to estimate the potential alcohol production is to multiply the Brix number by 0.55.

Let us consider that dry red wine. If it had 22 degrees Brix, you would use the following equation:

22.0 x 0.55 = 12.1% alcohol

The reverse is also true and it is the way you determine how much sugar you need in your must. Suppose you want to create a wine with 12.5% ABV, then use this equation:

12.50/0.55 = 22.70 degrees Brix

These numbers are estimates, as different yeasts will produce different results and can die off before achieving the potential alcohol level, which is why it is important to use the right yeast to produce a certain type of wine. If you receive juice or fresh grapes, you may not know what the sugar content is. You may want to purchase a hand refractor. It is a small device that uses light refraction to determine the sugar content of grape juice. Follow the instructions given in the equipment section or those included in the packaging.

If you find you need to add sugar, do so slowly; add about a ½ cup of sugar at a time to get the level of Brix you want. If the juice is too sweet, you can dilute it a little with water, although it is not recommended that you add more than 2 cups of water per gallon, or you could sacrifice the body and depth of your wine.

TIP If you want to add some residual sweetness to your wine after it is fermented, you may not want to add more refined sugar, as you risk fermentation. Consider using glycerin instead. It leaves a sweet taste, but it is non-fermentable. Do not use more than one once per gallon. Add it slowly and taste it before pouring too much in. In addition to adding sweetness, it can add body to your wine.

ACIDITY

Most grapes contain three types of acids: tartaric, malic, and citric. There is some lactic acid present, but in only small quantities. One of the things a winemaker must do when dealing with fresh juice or grapes is to test for total acidity (TA); this is the level of concentration of all the acids in grape juice. Total acidity is usually high when grapes are young and on the vine. It begins to decline as the grapes ripen and mature; this is especially true of malic acid.

TIP There are other trace acids in wines that are found in low quantities that contribute to the taste and complexity to a wine: oxalic, citramilic, gluconic, mucic, dimethylglyceric, ketoglutaric, galacturonic, glucuronic, and pyruvic acids.

A viticulturist, the person who runs the vineyard and makes decisions regarding growing techniques, decides what the total acid reading needs to be before grapes are harvested. This level is usually in the range of 6 to 9 grams per liter, or 0.6 percent to 0.9

percent. This number must be balanced with the sugar content of the grape in order to produce the best wine possible.

When you buy grape juice, the levels of sugar and total acid have already been determined for you. Most of the time, you will not need to make adjustments to the TA, but it is helpful to record in your winemaking journal so you can make adjustments later if you need to, or at least have some record so you can make adjustments for future batches.

Acid in a wine serves several important functions. First, it helps yeast during the fermentation process. It is not required, but it is preferred to ensure a healthy fermentation. This is probably due to the second reason that acid is needed in wine: It inhibits the growth of unwanted bacteria and wild yeasts. The lack of the proper level of acid increases the likelihood of spoilage and makes the cultivated yeast work harder as it competes for food.

Acid can also affect certain other chemical levels such as potassium and calcium salts that are responsible for the taste and color in a wine. Acid adds to the body, complexity, and tartness of wine. Being a home winemaker means you can decide what you want in the flavor of your wine. You may like a wine that is slightly more or less acidic. This is part of the joy of winemaking because you can be creative and in control of certain factors that can produce unique wines.

As the grape is growing on the vine, there are factors such as sun exposure and rainfall that can affect the acid concentration. A viticulturist must make a decision regarding when to pick grapes and may decide that all the other factors such as sugar levels are at their prime, but that they may need to make some slight adjustments to the total acid before fermentation. It is a balancing act that is sometimes tough because a winemaker cannot control factors such as sunlight and rainfall.

During the process of winemaking, the acid levels change: Lactic acid is formed while malic and tartaric acid decrease. Citric acid is usually only found in trace amounts in a finished wine. Tartaric acid is one of the most important acids in grapes and wine and gives a wine body and character, while malic acid can impart a tart, green apple flavor. This is the reason for secondary fermentation or malolactic fermentation. This is the process of converting harsh malic acid into a smoother, less biting lactic acid. There are those who are opposed to malolactic fermentation because it can impart a slight sour milk character to wine. In some styles of wine this might be desirable, but not in all.

TA (total acid) is the total concentration of all acids and is usually expressed as grams per liter or as a percentage of total acidity. An example is TA of 8.0 g/L or 0.80 percent total acidity. Even though it is measuring all the acids in a grape or wine, tartaric acid is used as a reference, so a TA measure is expressed as if it were only testing tartaric acid.

One of the ways to test acidity in juice or wine is titration. You can buy acid-testing kits from a home-winemaker supply store for usually less than $20. The process used in a titration testing kit is the neutralization of the acid content in a sample with a pH base solution. The amount of the solution or titrate that is needed to neutralize the acid determines the acid concentration.

You may determine that you need to make your wine more or less acidic through the process of acidification or de-acidification.

To raise the TA level, you will usually use an acid blend, or you can add other juices or wines. To lower acid levels, you can add some water, add an acid-reducing solution, and allow malolactic fermentation to occur, or cold-stabilize the wine and allow tartaric acid to crystallize and fall out.

Citric acid can be added to grape wine when there is too strong a malic acid to it. This will make the wine taste fresher. However, if too much is added, it can taste a little artificial. Citric acid can help prevent haze in wine but should be only added a ½ teaspoon at a time. In between additions, sample it.

Tartaric acid can be added to a wine that has a citric acid character to it. In some country wines that use citrus fruits, this addition is usually necessary to balance the taste and acidity.

Acetic acid exists in wine in small amounts, but should be eliminated or reduced if possible, as it is what leads to the spoilage of wine when certain bacteria begin to grow. This is what will turn wine into vinegar. Below is a table containing ballpark ranges of TA for different kinds of wine. The best way to determine the amount of acid you desire in wine is taste. Some people like slightly more bite to their wine. You are creating your own wine, so you can decide. Remember to write down what you do and keep in mind that you can always add a little more, but you cannot take away, so experiment slowly.

Sweet white grape wines (0.70 to 0.85%)
Sweet red grape wines (0.65 to 0.80%)
Sherry grape wines (0.50 to 0.60%)
Dry white grape wines (0.65 to 0.75%)
Dry red grape wines (0.60 to 0.70%)

Non-grape white wines (0.55 to 0.65%)
Non-grape red wines (0.50 to 0.60%)

You can increase the acid level by using the juice from citrus fruit. You may want to test the juice's TA before adding it so you have an idea of approximately how much you should be adding to the wine. When you are looking at a recipe for making a particular wine using juice or grapes, it may include instructions to add a teaspoon or two of acid blend. This is what the winemaker had to add to his or her wine based on the fruit he or she had available. Every crop of fruit will be different due to where it was grown, the climate, the soil conditions, the amount of sun exposure, and when the fruit was picked. Therefore, it is important to check the TA of the particular wine must you are working with before adding any acid blend.

Not all acid blends are created the same. It depends on the company that produces it what the percentages of acids are contained: tartaric, malic, and citric. Some of the common ratios are 50/25/25; 50/30/20; 40/30/30; and 40/40/20. If you want to know what type of acid blend you are thinking of purchasing, you can ask your supplier. You can also buy each type of acid separately and create your own blend based upon the ratio of your choosing. The most common ratio is 40/40/20, and by adding 3.9 grams per gallon, you will be able to raise the TA by 0.1 percent.

If you need to lower the acid level of your wine, you can add some of the following products:

Calcium carbonate is an additive will interact with tartaric acid. You can use this to lower the acid level from between 0.3 to 0.4 percent, but it is not recommended that you try to lower it more than this with calcium carbonate. The recommended amount to use is 2.5 grams per gallon, which will lower the TA by 0.1 percent.

When you use this product, you should allow the wine to age for at least six months. This allows the wine to produce calcium malate, formed by the calcium carbonate, to crystallize and drop out of the wine. The wine should then be cold-stabilized so that tartrate crystals do not form.

Potassium bicarbonate is another additive that can deacidify a wine that has too high an acid level, but should not be used to change the acidity more than 0.3 percent, or it can alter the flavor. The recommended amount to use for a gallon of wine is 3.4 grams, which will lower the acidity by 0.1 percent. Using this additive should be done in conjunction with cold stabilization. This process can lower the acid level up to 30 percent.

Potassium bitartrate is also known as cream of tartar, which you may have in your spice cabinet to use in certain types of baking. This additive helps in cold stabilization by promoting the production of tartrate crystals, which will fall out of the wine and lower the acid level. The recommended amount to use is 2 to 5 grams per gallon. Be sure that you completely stir and dissolve the powder.

PH LEVEL

This is very similar to TA in that it involves testing the acid level of a wine must — they are similar, but they are not the same. The pH level measures the potential of hydrogen (pH) in a solution. In contrast, TA measures the percentage of acid in a wine must. The pH determines the strength of acid in a solution and is based on a logarithmic scale, where 7 is the center or neutral point. This is the point where a solution is neither alkaline nor acidic. An example is regular water. All the numbers above the 7 are considered alkaline or basic, and all numbers below the 7 are acidic. The farther away from 7, the stronger the base or acid is considered to be. Because it is a logarithmic scale, each number is considered ten times stronger than the number preceding it. For instance, an acid with a pH of 4 is ten times stronger than an acid with the pH of 5. A pH of 10 is a 100 times stronger than a base with the pH of 8.

TA measures the *total* acids in a wine, whereas pH determines *how strong* these acids are. The pH and TA differ in that you may have the same amount of tartaric acid or malic acid in two different wines, equaling the TA. However, the pH would be lower in the malic acid wine, compared to the one that has the same amount of tartaric acid. The pH is the measure of the concentration of the number of hydrogen (H+) ions in a particular solution. Solutions with more H+ atoms are more acidic. The more H+ ions there are in a wine, the more they affect taste and other factors, This is called the effective acidity. The range that should be sought in most grapes, and therefore wines, is between 2.5 to 4.5 in a wine must. This is another measurement that is tested to allow viticulturists to decide when to pick grapes.

Wines with a lower pH tend to show better red color in red wines, and are more stable during aging; however, they will have less depth in taste and a weaker body then wines with a higher pH. Higher acid wines tend to age slower and will not spoil as often. It is important to monitor pH in wines you are making from juice and fresh grapes and make sure they stay in the safe range.

Simple pH-testing kits can give you an idea of the acid level in a wine. Insert the paper in a wine sample and use the included color chart to compare. This is a simple and inexpensive way to test pH but can be off by as much as 1 pH unit.

The more accurate way to test a wine's pH is using a pH meter. These sell for about $50 and are small, handheld meters that you will insert into a wine sample to give you a digital readout. These meters can read all pH levels from 0 to 14 but must be calibrated using solutions to make sure the readings are accurate. These solutions contain known pH levels. You will have to buy more of these calibration kits over time. The points in which the pH level should be tested are before fermentation, after fermentation, after malolactic fermentation, and after cold stabilization.

CASE STUDY: SPOTLIGHT ON
ADVANTAGE BEER & WINE
SUPPLIES

Mike Walkup, Co-owner
Advantage Beer & Wine Supplies
2508 US Highway 70 SW
Hickory, NC 28602
828-328-3140
www.advantagebeerandwine.com

"We have been in business of supplying winemaking supplies for five years. My partner tried a wine kit, and we were instantly hooked. It was really good wine for a fraction of the price it would cost to buy wine retail at a store.

We are different from some other wine supply stores in that we make all the wines we sell kits for in the store. This way, customers have a chance to taste the wine before they buy the kit. We have a tasting bar, and we also sell many of our kit wines. We had to get our ABC (Alcohol Beverage Control Board) and TTB (Alcohol and Tobacco Tax and Trade Bureau) licenses to serve and produce wine.

We sell beer and wine kits at the store, and even allow a local homebrew society to meet here after hours. We feel you can get the same great quality from home winemaking as you can buy it at a retailer."

CHAPTER 5

Wine from Grapes

"Come quickly! I am tasting stars!"

— Dom Pérignon (after tasting champagne for the first time)

O nce you have created some wines using grape juice, you may want even more control by buying grapes to make wine. If you do not own a crusher, destemmer, or press, you might need to borrow these items or use them at a winery. There are some wineries that have cooperatives that allow members to use their equipment for a nominal fee. Look on the Internet to see if there is one in your area.

You can also buy grapes that have already been destemmed, crushed, and prepared for fermentation — but you will still need to press the grapes. If you belong to a wine club, you may also have access to community equipment, and some online clubs make trips to vineyard-crushing facilities once a year at harvest time.

RED WINE MACERATION

Maceration is one of the key differences between red wine and white wine. This is the process of allowing red wine to sit on the grape skins for a period of time at the beginning of fermentation. This is not done in the production of a white wine. Allowing the red wine to sit on the wine solids allows the skins to release color, taste, body, and depth into the juice. The compounds that do this are tannins. The amounts of tannins that are released into a wine depend on the maceration technique that is used.

The difference in techniques is in the maceration time, temperature, and cap management. The cap is the crust of grape solids that float to the top of the wine must during maceration. The longer the period of maceration, the deeper the color and the more full-bodied the flavor imparted to the wine must.

The amount of tannin extraction is high during the first few days of maceration and will begin to slow over time. However, the color extraction will be fast at first and will stop altogether after Day 10. In order to get the maximum tannin extraction, you want to extend the period as long as possible while stopping fermentation from taking over. Fermentation will slow down and even stop the extraction process.

The temperature of the must will raise the temperature to 90 degrees F or greater. This temperature increase can lead to a premature stalling of the fermentation. The way to prevent this is by using a maceration technique called cold-soak pre-fermentation. It is important to keep the grapes cool prior to maceration and should be refrigerated. After the grapes have been crushed, sealed bags of ice are added to the must. You must stir the must every few hours and replace the ice as needed. 100 mg/L of potassium metabisulfite should also be added to retard any fermentation.

Another technique that is used during maceration is punching down the cap. This is done with a sanitized stick, and the skins are pushed back down into the juice. This allows more surface area for extraction and prevents spoilage. You can create a punching device using a broom handle to which you attach a square piece of oak. Make sure this oak square is not wider than the maceration vessel.

During maceration, be sure to keep the vessel covered to prevent any bugs from being attracted to the fruit and juice. You can macerate in a fermentation vessel or two and place the lids with a fermentation lock attached on top. It is better if you can use larger vessels that are wider. You will have more extraction with a greater surface area between the juice and the solids.

CO_2 produced by fermentation creates a barrier of gas that prevents spoilage. In the process of cold soaking, no fermentation is occurring and therefore no CO_2 gas is being produced. You may want to inject some CO_2 gas into the vessel under the lid. You can buy small canisters of CO_2 from a winemaking supplier or from a gas company. A note of caution: CO_2 can be hazardous in high concentration, causing breathing difficulty, light-headedness and, in extreme cases, suffocation.

Another technique used during maceration to ensure the maximum extraction is called "pumping over." This involves using an electric pump to move the juice over the top of the cap. This has the added benefit of cooling the wine; however, this should not be overdone, as it can oxidize the wine. Twenty seconds at a time is sufficient for home-winemaking purposes. These pumps can be rather expensive, especially if you only intend on making 5 to 6 gallons of wine at a time. You can manually pump over by allowing juice to run into a bucket from the spigot and then taking that wine and pouring it over the top. You can do this three to four times to get the same effect as an electric pump. Make sure you sanitize the bucket.

Once maceration is complete, you can remove the juice into a fermenter and transfer the solids or pomace to a press. The juice from maceration is called "free run wine" (vin de goutte). Once the free run juice has been removed, you can then press the pomace (grape skins) to extract more juice. This is called "press wine" (vin de presse). You may chose to mix these two wines or make two separate wines that can be blended or even bottled separately. Be careful not to break any of the grape seeds, as this can impart a bitter flavor to your wine.

Under the instructions section, you will find simple step-by-step instructions. For this first recipe, I have written out more detailed instructions, and you can refer to these. You may decide to condition your water or add clarifiers at the end.

Another way to increase extraction during maceration is to add a bit of pectic enzyme at the time the grapes are crushed. This breaks down the cell walls in the grapes and allows more juice and pigments to escape. The recommended amount to use is ½ ounce per gallon of wine. Do not use pectic enzyme if there are stems on the grapes, as it will release harsh flavors.

Note: You will see two forms of measuring alcohol content in your wine: by measuring original and final gravities (OG and FG), and by measuring "Brix." You will see both of these beneath each wine recipe name; you can use either method. Be sure to measure your potential alcohol level before adding sugar to any recipe; adding too much sugar will make your alcohol content too high. Usually, you will not need to add sugar when creating wine from fruit.

Cabernet Sauvignon

(This recipe can be used for most any other red grape wine)
Yield 1 gallon/3.8 L
OG = 1.100 FG = 0.995 ABV = 14%
Original Brix (27.04) - Final Brix (1.80) = 25.24 x 0.55 = 14%

Ingredients:

12 lbs. Cabernet Sauvignon grapes (Check your original sugar levels and make note of this)
Sugar or other sweetener to bring must to 24 Brix or 1.10 OG
3 Campden (sulfite) tablets
1 tsp. yeast nutrient
1 packet wine yeast
2 tsp. pectic enzyme
Water (enough to make 1 gallon of wine must)
Standard winemaking equipment
Nylon bag/cheesecloth
1-gallon carboy

Instructions:

Day 1

1. Determine ahead of time whether you want a sweet wine or a dry wine. You will want to also determine whether you want a high alcohol wine or low. If you wish to make a dry wine, ferment the juice until it is "dry," or close to

0 Brix or 0% residual alcohol. If you wish to have some sweetness, ferment to a residual sugar level of about 1 to 3 percent.

2. Purchase or pick wine grapes. Regular eating grapes are not normally fit for making wine because they do not contain enough tannins, and the skins are too thin. The exception is Concord grapes, mentioned in the basic recipe. You can buy wine grapes from farmers' markets or from local vineyards. It takes about 12 lbs. of grapes to produce 1 gallon of wine. If you cannot find Cabernet Sauvignon grapes, then you can use some other similar red wine grape. The first day you will be processing the grapes, whether you bought or picked them.

3. When you get the grapes home, thoroughly rinse them. Removing any bad grapes or debris. If you allow the grapes to sit for a couple of hours, most insects will make their way to the top of the grapes, which will make it easier to dispose of them.

4. Remove all the stems by hand and discard them. You should not allow any stems into your wine, as they may impart a bitter taste.

5. Crush the grapes. Do not use a food processor, as the seeds can impart bitter and undesirable flavors. You can crush the grapes by hand if it is a small batch or place them in a small fruit press. If you do use a press, do not press them all the way — just break the skins. You can also choose to crush the grapes like your ancestors did: by stomping them. Sanitize your feet well, then place the

grapes in a plastic fermentation bucket and jump in with your bare feet. The goal is to break the skins to allow the juice to seep out. Catch the event on film.

6. After you have crushed the grapes and the juice has begun to flow, you should perform an acid and sugar test. This is not necessary to make wine. I include it here as a placeholder for when you wish perform these types of tests. These readings are important if you want to have complete control over the final results. These tests will determine sugar and acid levels, though they will not guarantee you will have an award-winning wine. In order to perform these tests, you will need to extract some of the juice from the fermenter. Use the results to decide whether you will need to add more sugar or possibly dilute the mixture.

7. You can raise the sugar level by adding small amounts of sugar (by the cup), or you can use grape juice concentrate. You will want to do this slowly and check the readings before adding any more sugar or juice. Remember that you can always add more, but once the sugar or juice is mixed in, you cannot take it away. Determine ahead of time whether you want a sweet wine or dry wine. You will want to also determine whether you want a high- or low-alcohol wine. Sugar controls how sweet the wine will be and what the potential alcohol level will be. Once you have determined what kind of wine you want to create, choose the right yeast. Most wine yeast can withstand an alcohol content of 12% to 14%. If you want sweeter wine, add more sugar than the yeast can convert to alcohol. For a drier wine, have

just enough sugar. If you want a higher alcohol content, then raise the specific gravity and choose a higher alcohol-tolerant yeast strain.

8. Adjusting the acid level will affect the mouth feel of a wine. Too little acid will make it have a soft and diluted mouth feel, whereas too much acid can negatively affect the yeast and create too tart a wine. Your target acid should be 0.6 to 0.7 percent in red wines and 0.7 to 0.8 percent in whites.

9. Once you have determined your wine is ready for fermentation, kill off any wild yeasts or bacteria that can negatively affect your wine by turning it into vinegar, stopping fermentation, or ruining the taste of your finished product. The simplest way to sterilize your wine must is to add sulfites. As I have mentioned in this book, I do not recommend over-sulfiting your wine. Add an average of ½ teaspoon of metabisulphite for every 5 to 6 gallons of wine. I use Campden tablets, which are measures of compressed sulfite powder. If you use Campden tablets, crush them by hand, use the back of a spoon against a tabletop, or use a mortar and pestle.

10. The largest difference in a red wine is that you will be fermenting the wine with the skins still present. This fermentation should be slow, so cool the must. A simple way to cool the must is to place sealable plastic bags filled with ice in the must. Before placing the bags in the must, make sure you have sanitized them. You do not have to do this, but you should place the must in a dark,

cool place. The must will need to rest 24 hours in order for the sulphite to "gas off."

11. After 24 hours, you will pitch (add) your yeast into the must. You will use one packet for up to 6 gallons of wine.

Days two to 12

1. You are ready to move onto the maceration stage of red winemaking. This is also referred to as fermenting on the skins. You want this part of the fermentation process to go slowly. Replace your ice bags if you are using them. The grape skins float to the top of the vessel and form a cap or crust over the juice. Push the skins back into the must to get the most color and tannins possible for a colorful, full-bodied red wine. This is called 'punching down the cap.' Punch down the cap by hand or use a paddle or spoon. Whatever you decide to use, make sure you sanitize your hands and equipment.

2. The length of time the wine macerates is totally up to you. The longer you leave the skins, the more tannins are released. Tannins give a certain mouth feel and can feel slightly astringent on the tongue. You do not want too many tannins, or it will be unpalatable. Too little tannin, and the wine will be considered weak or not very complex. You will need to taste the wine in order to make decide when it is at the right level of astringency. There is a window for the length as far as the wine color is concerned. For up to seven days, the wine will deepen in color. After seven days, the color will begin to get

lighter. The wine will continue to lighten, but tannins will continue to be released.

3. If you want the best-tasting wine possible, do not press the skins when you remove them. The juice in your fermenter will create the highest quality wine. The juice you press from the grapes will be weaker and pales in comparison. You could decide to create two different wines; the wine created from pressing the grapes is referred to as second-run wine. Unless you have a lot of juice from the first run, you may want to press all the juice from the grapes and mix it with the first-run juice. The result will not be bad wine; it is just juice that is not as complex as a first run wine without the grapes pressed.

4. A small press for the grape skins can be helpful — a small investment in order to save the trouble of making a mess. Add the crushed grapes to your press, and press the juice either into your primary vessel or in a second vessel if you are making second-run wine. Make sure everything is sanitized before you begin pressing. Do not ratchet the press all the way down because you could crush the seeds, which can give a bitter taste to your wine. Dry out the grape skins and use them as fire kindling, or compost them in your garden.

5. Make sure you do not have too much headroom in your vessel. You can add more wine or grape juice of the same variety to make up the difference. Unless noted in the recipe, do not dilute it with water, or this can dilute the taste of your wine. If you have some extra juice, seal it in jugs without adding yeast to top off your wine during

racking. During the next period of fermentation — days 13 through 39 — there is not much to do except keep the wine in a temperature-controlled area and take a hydrometer/refractometer reading every three to five days.

Days 40 to 60

1. The wine should begin to slow fermentation and be completed between 40 and 60 days from the time you started the wine. This includes primary and secondary or malolactic fermentation. During this period of time, it is recommended that once primary fermentation begins to slow down, you should rack the wine into a carboy to begin secondary fermentation. You will know it is stopping by how rapidly the bubbling is in the fermentation lock. Secondary formation mellows the wine and makes it smoother to drink. This is the time when different unwanted chemicals are moved by the yeast such as diacetyl, acetylaldehyde, and some sulphur compounds. During secondary fermentation, you will begin to see a sediment form. This is called trub (pronounced "troob") and is made up of dead yeast and other proteins. You will begin to see the wine become clearer and easier to see through. It is at this time that you can add clarifiers to draw out even more proteins that are suspended in the wine to the bottom of the carboy. Malolactic fermentation also refers to the process of removing malic acid. This is accomplished when lactic acid bacteria consumes the malic acid for energy. This process can occur naturally in wines, or you may choose to add lactic acid bacteria during secondary fermentation.

2. Once fermentation has completely ceased, you may choose to bottle or age the wine. You will know that fermentation has ceased by consistent hydrometer readings. In the recipes in this book, you will see "FG" above the ingredients list. This is the final gravity and gives an idea of what to look for as a final specific gravity reading. You choose to add stabilizers such as Campden tablets to ensure the wine will not begin fermentation in the bottle or while aging.

WHITE WINES

There is not much difference between making a white wine and red wine. The greatest difference in the process occurs in the beginning. Instead of fermenting on the skins, the skins are pressed just after they are crushed. The skins never touch the fermenting must. This gives white wine a different character because it contains less tannin, and it does not have the red ruby color.

Otherwise, the process is exactly the same.

Common white wine varietals:
- Albariño/Alvarinho
- Chardonnay
- Chenin Blanc
- Gewürztraminer
- Muscat
- Pinot Blanc
- Pinot Gris/Pinot Grigio
- Riesling
- Sauvignon Blanc
- Sémillon
- Viognier

You can try some of these varietals on your own to get some practice making wine. The following is a recipe for a Chardonnay. This recipe can be converted to make just about any other white grape wine.

Chardonnay Wine

Yield 5 gallons (19L)

OG = 1.09 FG = 1.014 ABV = 10%

Original Brix (21.10) - Final Brix (3.10) = 18 x 0.55 = 10% ABV

60 to 75 lbs. Chardonnay grapes
½ tsp. pectic enzyme
17 Campden tablets
1 packet of Red Star Montrachet yeast
3 tsp. yeast nutrient
3 tsp. oak mar (flavor), or 2 cups oak chips, or 3 oak staves (available at your wine making supplier)
1 package of malolactic culture
Standard winemaking equipment
Crusher (or you may crush the grapes by hand or foot)
Fruit press

Instructions:

1. Clean and sanitize everything. Crush the gapes after removing bugs, debris, and bad clusters. Add pectic enzyme to the grapes. Let sit for two hours.

2. Press the grapes (with fruit press). Add five Campden tablets to grape juice. Let sit 12 hours.

3. Take readings of the acid and sugar content and make any necessary adjustments. Make a yeast starter by adding yeast to warm water and allowing it to sit for 30 minutes. Pitch yeast and add nutrient and oak mar or other oak sources to the juice. Rock the fermenter to mix and aerate.

4. Cover top of fermenter with a trash bag. Make sure there is headspace for fermentation of about 20 percent. After three days, wine should be vigorously fermenting. Allow it to ferment two more weeks. After fermentation looks like it has slowed down, rack into carboy.

5. Add malolactic culture, following the instructions on the packet.

6. Take hydrometer/refractometer readings, and when the reading is below 1.000 or 1 Brix, then fermentation should be complete. When it reaches level, add five more Campden tablets to the must and rack.

7. Place the fermenter in a cool place for three to six months. Continue to rack every month until it is clear. During each racking, add three more Campden tablets.

8. If needed, you can use other clarifiers such as Isinglass to clear the wine.

9. When wine is clear and acceptable to your taste, then pour into bottles.

10. Allow the wine to age for another three months before drinking.

Aging

After the readings on the hydrometer or refractometer are stable, you may choose to skip to bottling. However, aging a wine will make a smooth, mellow, and complex flavor. It does take some willpower. Many home winemakers want to try to drink a wine as quickly as possible. If you can just wait, the taste will only improve. You do want to make sure you have racked the wine off the sediment or "lees" because they can begin to decay in a process called autolysis, which will alter the flavor of your wine. Even during the aging period, you may occasionally rack the wine into another carboy if you see sediment forming.

You may choose to age your wine in an oak barrel. Some people do not like the taste of oak, while others will swear by it. It is purely a matter of taste and preference. Remember, this is your wine, and you get to decide how it will turn out. You do have the option of adding oak chips to the carboy instead of barrel-aging your wine. I have used this low-cost alternative with great success.

Barrel aging:

Different winemakers age in barrels, and each seems to have their own preference of the types of barrels, what kind of wine goes into those barrels, and how long they should be aged.

"We use French Oak barrels that are heavily toasted to age our reds. We do not oak barrel age our whites or Rose; they are aged in stainless-steel vessels."

— Drew Renegar; Allison Oaks Vineyards

• • • • • • • • • • •

"We barrel-age all our red wines because they need to breathe. We also barrel-age our Chardonnay. We use medium-toasted French Oak for at least 60 percent of our wines. The cost of these barrels runs about $1,050, and we use them about five years. We use American Oak for about 30 percent of our barrel aging, and the last 10 percent are in Hungarian Oak barrels. We are barrel-aging our wine about a year for most of our wines and up to three years for our reserve wines."

— Mark Terry, general manager and winemaker;
Westbend Vineyards

• • • • • • • • • • •

"Our reds are barrel-aged, as is our Chardonnay and Viognier. Ninety-five percent of the barrels are French Oak. We chose those because they tend to soften the wine, while American and Hungarian are a little harsher to the palate."

— Steve Shepard, vintner and general manager;
RayLen Vineyard & Winery

During the process of aging wine, some evaporation occurs. This is completely natural — however, it creates headspace. This can give bad bacteria a place to form, which can ruin your wine. You can add a few cups of a similar wine without affecting the taste of the wine you are aging. It is better to use wine than grape juice because the sugars in raw juice can cause fermentation to reoccur.

With white wines, it is important to ensure your wine is aged in a very cool and preferably dark environment; strive to keep your wine at 55 degrees F. Anyone can have his or her own private cave in which to age wine. Try to create the effect of a cave by placing your wine in a basement or even in a crawl space under your home. If you seal your vessel well, you should not have to worry about any insects getting into your wine. As long as your wine is cold and stable, you can seal a vessel without fear of its exploding.

You may want to check your wine for taste and character as it ages. Try to keep this to a minimum because you risk contamination every time you unseal a vessel. Any time you remove wine, you should fill up your container to reduce headspace.

At the six-month mark, you may want to consider racking the wine, especially if any sediment has formed. This is a good time to test and taste your wine.

If your wine smells bad or is not clearing, you may want to check the troubleshooting chapter at the end of this book. There is always the possibility that a wine will go bad. Most of the time, a wine goes bad because of bad sanitation procedures. Sanitizing and cleaning everything will reduce the risk of contaminated wine significantly.

You may decide to filter your wine before bottling. This is usually unnecessary, especially because the scale of winemaking most home winemakers create is small. Remember that filtering can remove the good with the bad; your wine could become pale and flat-tasting.

"It is necessary for many commercial wineries to polish their wines with filtering. We use a .45 micron filter on our wines."

— Mark Terry, general manager and winemaker;
Westbend Vineyards

• • • • • • • • • •

"If you are making wine from a kit, you will not need to filter it unless you really want to. Racking the wine and putting in the correct clarifiers usually will do the job."

— Mike Walkup, co-owner;
Advantage Beer & Wine Supplies

Make sure there are no changes in your hydrometer/refractometer readings. Once you are sure your wine is ready, it is time to bottle your wine. Rack the wine off lees and into a primary fermenter bucket. This is now your bottling bucket. Attach a tube from the bottom spigot with a bottle filler at the end of the tubing. Make sure there is no fermentation lock on the lid. Filling the bottle will create a vacuum that can pull the water or sulfite solution right from the fermentation lock into your wine. Make sure you have plenty of sanitized bottles ready to be filled. Once you fill them, cork them immediately. The less time your wine is exposed to the air, the better. Oxygen can begin to break down and oxidize your wine. This can lead to a metallic, flat taste that can only be cured by pouring otherwise perfectly good wine down the drain. After bottling, be sure to allow the wine to settle a few weeks before opening.

More tips on aging

Some people have questions about how long they should age their wine. Here are some suggestions based on the type of wine you are aging. Keep in mind that if you are using barrels, you can use a barrel that you aged white wine in for either a white or red wine. If you age red wine in a barrel, you can only use it for red wines from then on.

1. If you are allowing full-bodied red wines to age, they should be allowed to mature for at least a year. If you have the patience, allow them to mature for two to three years. Unless you have an iron will and great patience, you probably will not wait that long.

2. If you are creating light red and rose wines, then you should allow them to mature six months to a full year before drinking.

3. If you are aging a full-flavored white wine, try to age them for a minimum of six months; a year is better.

If you decide to age a light, fruity white wine, you should age it for at least three months, but six months is even better.

Blending wines

"Blending wine creates a wine that is a sum greater than its parts."
— Mike Helton, vintner; Hanover Park Vineyard

The United States is one of the only countries that names wines according to their varietal, such as Chardonnay or Merlot. In Europe, wines are named after the regions they come from, such as Chianti or Boudreaux. Many times blended wines are given the names of these regions according to the types of wines they usually produce. For instance, Chianti is made from grapes in the Chianti region in Italy. It is based on a certain recipe for blending wine in that region.

The idea behind blending wines is that the whole is greater than the sum of its parts. There are some varietals that blend together well to create a better wine then the assorted wines would be if they stood alone.

I created a Chianti wine that won a gold medal at an international wine competition. The recipe consisted of 70 percent Sangiovese,

15 percent Canaiolo, and 15 percent Malvasia Bianca. There are two ways in which this could be created:

- The first way is to blend the juices in the proportions mentioned and ferment them together as one wine. This method of juice blending is easier if you have the proportions already worked out through someone else's recipe or through experience creating blended wines in the past.

- The other way is to create three different wines and then blend them together. This method gives you more control over the final result. Take small amounts of the three wines and mix them together in different proportions. Write down the results with the exact proportions you used.

I recommend you experiment using the second method. If you try to blend at the beginning of fermentation, you could ruin the whole batch. Some blends do not turn out to be palatable.

I recommend trying up to five combinations at a time (a tasting of a few different wines at a time is often referred to as a "flight"). Your palate cannot truly discern the taste of the wine if you try a larger flight. The tannins and alcohol overwork your tongue and taste buds. If you find a blend you like, put it aside overnight. The next day, try the combination again and see if you still like the blend. Once you have found a blend you like, you can then mix the wines in the exact same proportions you did when mixing small amounts.

Do not mix wines before you have tried them out in small proportions. You will work hard to create wines, and working too quickly can ruin it all.

Another type of blending that is used by wineries worldwide is mixing different wines from different regions. The wines can be the same varietal but have slightly different qualities caused by soil, water, or climate. By mixing different wines, these slight differences will cancel each other out and create a blend that exemplifies the best characteristics of its variety. In order for wineries to produce consistent-tasting wine, they often use this type of blending. They will often reserve wine from different vintages and use it to blend with wine to bring it closer to the standard measurements of wine they produce year after year.

CASE STUDY: SPOTLIGHT ON HANOVER PARK VINEYARD

Michael Helton, Vintner
Hanover Park Vineyard
1927 Courtney-Huntsville Road
Yadkinville, NC 27055
www.hanoverparkwines.com

It was after Michael and Amy Helton's 1996 honeymoon in southern France that they developed a love for wine. By December of that year, they opened Hanover Park Vineyard, located in the Yadkin Valley of North Carolina. They were working as artists and teachers, but they thought they would take a chance in turning an old farm into a working vineyard.

The Heltons started slowly by volunteering at another winery in order to learn the craft. Finally, in 1997, the Heltons began planting their vineyard based on what Mike had learned. In 1998, Mike began making homemade wines to get a feel for the process. It was a new retirement venture, and he was impressed and encouraged by his early results. He even has some of the homemade wine equipment sitting around the winery. As the vines grew, the 1897 home was transformed into a winery; in 2000, they added a tasting room.

Mike did not have any formal training in winemaking or viticulture; instead, he was self-taught. He asked other vineyards owners, read every book he could get his hands on and joined winemaker forums. To further his education and reconnect to the place where they originally fell in love with wine, the Heltons returned to the south of France in 2002, except this time they made appointments with French winemakers to learn the traditional French methods and blends. He liked the French and other European wines because they were so easy to drink. They were not an "acquired taste;" rather, they were smooth and accessible. He wanted to create this same sort of wine at home.

Mike continued to work for a number of years as the winery got on its feet. He thought it was important to keep his day job while getting the business going. He began by planting 4 acres and buying the other grapes he needed those first few years from other local grape growers. He now has about 8 acres of vines growing. His commitment is to create a great North Carolina wine using locally grown grapes.

While Mike was learning the ropes at the winery, Amy retired from teaching in 2004 so she could take over the tasting room, plan all events, and develop a marketing and branding program.

CHAPTER 6

Common Winemaking Mistakes and How to Fix Them

"Penicillin cures, but wine makes people happy."

— Alexander Fleming (1881-1955), discoverer of penicillin

There are a number of things that can go wrong while making a wine at home. That is part of the challenge, and you will have to be creative at times in overcoming these while still producing world-class homemade wines. In this chapter, I have included some of the most common errors. I have made hundreds of wines, and I am still referring to this list. If you remember nothing else, remember that having sanitized hands and equipment will solve over 90 percent of the problems you will encounter when creating your own wine.

"I use sulfite tablets to wash the fruit and kill all the wild bacteria. I use one to two tablets per gallon of water. I use potassium metabisulfite Campden tablets. Other than that, I don't use chemicals. Because I don't use chemicals or charcoal filters, my wine contains settlings, which are "lees" or remnants of the pulp. I continually strain my wine (even rebottle it) to remove these. After two years, the wine is typically completely clear. Commercial wine makers will use chemicals so there are no settlings."

— Richard Schlicht, home winemaker

NO. 1 — MY WINE IS TOO ACIDIC

You may notice that the wine has a very tart taste after you have fermented it. You may need to cold-stabilize it. This means you will have to store your wine in a place that is close to freezing. You do not want to freeze your wine; you just want to make it very cold (about 38 degrees F). The acid molecules will crystallize and fall to the bottom of the fermenter. You will need to rack the wine off these acid crystals. Taste your wine after racking. You may need to repeat the process again.

NO. 2 — MY WINE WILL NOT STOP FERMENTING

If it seems that your wine is still bubbling, then you should check the SG. There could still be sugar left. Stir the wine well a couple of times. If there are no other off colors or odors, do not worry. Just sit tight and be patient. If the reading states that your wine has finished fermenting, this could mean there is just extra CO_2 gas being released. This can happen if there was a slow fermentation. Stir the wine vigorously to release any extra gas that may be trapped.

NO. 3 — MY WINE HAS BUBBLES

Carbonation can be caused by refermentation, or your wine could be infected. You can stir the wine and de-gas it. If it has been infected, try to add some sulfites. You may have to discard the wine if the flavor, color, or aroma changes.

NO. 4 — MY WINE IS "BLAH"

A bland-tasting wine can be caused by the lack of acid or tannin in your wine. You can add 1 teaspoon of lemon juice or some strong black tea to your wine to try to balance the flavor. If this does not work, then your wine may not be salvageable. Make sure in future batches that you add enough acid blend at the beginning of your winemaking process. You can add ⅛ teaspoon of tartaric acid to the wine and stir. Allow it to sit for two to four hours, after which you can taste the wine to see if it has improved. If it has not improved enough, you can add another ⅛ teaspoon of tartaric acid, making sure to stir it in vigorously. You can continue this process a few more times to see if it improves the wine significantly. Another option is to blend it with another wine that is slightly acidic.

NO. 5 — MY WINE IS CLOUDY OR HAZY

Your wine can become hazy to look through due to protein matter, pectin, starch, or metallic contamination. Haziness does not make it spoiled unless there is a foul smell accompanying it; it is more about the aesthetic of the wine you have created. You want it to look as good as it tastes. Most of the time, yeast will remove protein haze during fermentation. Sometimes, racking alone will not remove cloudiness from your wine. Never bottle a hazy wine. It cannot be treated in the bottle, and the haziness will not clear up. If you did bottle hazy wine, you will have to dump it back into the fermenter, treat it, then rebottle it.

A simple way to clear your wine before bottling is to add a little egg white, or you can bake some eggshells until they become dry. Crush the eggshells into the wine and allow the proteins to be drawn to the bottom. You can then rack your wine again.

You can buy a number of different clearing agents mentioned earlier in this book; try different ones to see if it improves your wine. Do not try to filter your wine, as this will not clear haziness. Filtering only improves already cleared wine. If there are fining agents in the wine, they will block most wine filters and make them ineffective.

Some country wines contain pectin that can make a wine hazy. That is why many of them have the inclusion of a pectic enzyme that will break down pectin and prevent haziness from occurring. If you were creating a wine using other types of fruits or vegetables and you boiled those ingredients, your wine may develop a pectin haze. You can test your wine to determine if it has a pectin haze by extracting some wine and adding 3 ounces of methylated spirits. If there is pectin present, it will create jelly-like clots or strings.

Methylated spirits is also called denatured alcohol and is used as a solvent and the fuel for camp stoves. It usually contains 10 percent methanol. It is very toxic to consume. You can buy methylated spirits from hardware and camping stores.

If you have determined that it is a pectin haze problem, then extract a cup of the wine and add a teaspoon of pectic enzyme to it. Put this sample in a warm environment of between 70 and 80 degrees F for four hours. Pour the liquid, through a piece of cheesecloth, back into the wine. Keep the wine in a warm place for four to five days and the pectin haze should clear.

If you find that the pectin haze has not completely cleared, you can strain the wine through cheesecloth and filter it. If this still does not solve the haze problem, then there is another reason other than pectin that is causing the problem.

The best way to prevent a pectin haze is to add pectic enzymes to the wine must at least 12 hours before pitching the yeast. The regular rate is about one teaspoon of pectic enzyme per gallon, but in some wines, this may increase to 1 ½ teaspoons per gallon.

Starch can also be a source of haze in a wine. This is caused by using ingredients such as grains or tubers boiled to make wine. If you used these types of ingredients, the likely culprit for a hazy wine is starch. You can determine if starch is causing the problem in your wine by adding about 5 drops of iodine to a wine sample. If the wine turns a dark indigo-blue color, then there is starch present.

If you have determined that it is starch that is affecting your wine, you can treat it by adding Amylase or Amylozyme 100, both of which can be purchased at a home winemaking equipment supplier. Amylase works on starch the way that pectic enzyme works on pectin. Collect 1 cup of wine per gallon. For example, if you have 5 gallons, you would draw off 5 cups. For each cup, add 1 teaspoon of Amylase and stir. Allow this mixture to sit in a warm setting (70 to 80 degrees F) for four hours and stir it once an hour.

On the fourth hour, pour the mixture through a piece of cheese-cloth back into the wine. Allow the wine to sit for another four to five days, after which the haze should be gone. If you find the haze is still there, pour the wine through a piece of cheesecloth and then filter it.

If you decide to use Amylozyme 100, the procedure is different. Pour 1 tablespoon of Amylozyme 100 per 1 gallon of wine and allow the wine to sit for a week at 70 to 75 degrees F. This should clear the starch haze.

When you are creating country recipes that call for ingredients such as parsnips, potatoes, turnips, grains, apples, pears, or any starchy material, you can count on there being a starch haze. Most of the recipes will warn you to drip dry and lightly squeeze the liquid from the bag. If you press hard on the nylon bag or cheese-cloth, then you will get a greater starch haze, so be aware of this when creating these types of wines.

If you find that none of these solutions have helped your wine and you have racked it at least six times and allowed to clear for a month, then you may just have cloudy wine without a specific

MAKING WINE

at home and with the professionals

Home Winemaking Photos by the Hewitt Family Vineyard

Napa Valley Cabernet vineyard, Calistoga, California.

Cabernet grape clusters at Hewitt Family Vineyard in Calistoga, California.

Harvest crewmembers Mark Brandi, Maureen Brandi, Crystal Acker, George Salvaggio Jr., Zeena Janowsky, and Gary Blackman pick Merlot grapes at Hewitt Family Vineyard.

Harvest crewmembers Crystal Acker, along with others, crush and de-stem their grapes at Hewitt Family Vineyard.

Harvest crewmembers Annette Salvaggio and Crystal Acker pick Cabernet grapes at Hewitt Family Vineyard.

Harvest crewmembers Frank Hewitt, along with others, pour Merlot grapes into a machine that will crush and de-stem them.

Pacific Star Winery in Mendocino County, California.

Harvest crewmembers Amy Gerbus and Dave Goulette weigh grapes to estimate the juice content.

Harvest crewmembers Zeena Janowsky, Annette Salvaggio, and others place the Merlot grapes into the wine press to crush and de-stem them.

Wine must is stirred in buckets. This helps mix the juice with the skins and aerates it to begin fermentation. After being stirred, the wine must is transferred to the wine press.

Open fermentation of red wines at Pacific Star Winery, in Mendocino County, California.
George Salvaggio Sr. looks at the grapes while visiting the winery for a tasting.

Wine press filled with wine must.

Harvest crewmember Crystal Acker places
must into the wine press to press out the wine.

Harvest crewmember Amy Maestri presses
the must into wine.

Free-run wine pours into a bucket before the must has been pressed.

Crewmember George Salvaggio Jr. tastes the pressed wine for quality control.

Harvest crewmembers George Salvaggio Jr. and Mark Brandi clean the 60-gallon barrel during the racking and bottling stage.

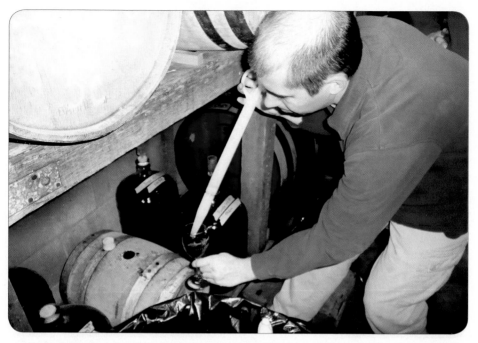

Harvest crewmember Mike Acker uses a wine thief to draw wine out of a 5-gallon barrel for tasting purposes.

Once the bottles are filled with wine, Annette Salvaggio (pictured above), places a cork in the bottle to seal it.

George Salvaggio Jr. uses a gravity siphon to bottle the wine.

Mike Acker and Michael Turner bottle wine.

Amy Gerbus, George Salvaggio Jr., and George Salvaggio Sr. enjoy their finished wine at a harvest party.

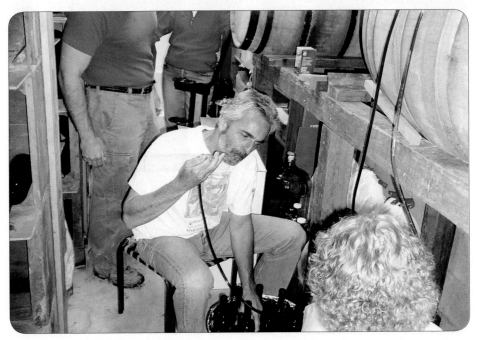

George Salvaggio Jr., Mike Acker, Crystal Acker, and Al Brandi form a wine-bottling assembly line.

Autumn King table grapes at the Hewitt Family Vineyard.

Award-winning Hewitt Family Vineyard home brews, created by Inger Hewitt.

Harvest crewmembers Michael Turner, Crystal Acker, Mike Acker, Annette Salvaggio (daughter of Inger Hewitt), Inger Hewitt, and Frank Hewitt pose in a vineyard at the Hewitt Family Vineyard located in Calistoga, California.

Once the wine has been bottled, it is placed in a cellar so the wine can age in a climate-controlled environment.

Winery Photos by John Peragine

If you plan to open your own winery, take some tips from Westbend Vineyards, with their well-stocked and attractive tasting room.

This apple and fruit crusher on sale at Advantage Beer & Wine Supplies has a hand crank to crush fruit. A bucket is placed below the crusher to catch the shredded fruit and juice.

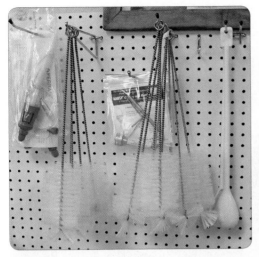

Advantage Beer & Wine Supplies displays a collection of equipment-cleaning tools. Pictured here are bottle brushes and a brass fitting that is fastened to a faucet to spray water into bottles and carboys for cleaning. These hang alongside a number of different-sized spoons to stir wine.

A home winemaker can use a hair dryer to shrink capsules onto bottles, but at Hanover Park Vineyard, this machine does the same job. A capsule is placed on the bottle, and the top of the bottle is inserted in the hole. Next to the capsule shrinker is a roll of labels, ready to be glued to bottles.

Advantage Beer & Wine Supplies has a number of wine bottle labels that can be fastened to your bottle using a little water. There are different labels according to your style and type of wine in the bottle.

Some wine can be aged for months in stainless-steel vessels instead of oak barrels. Westbend Vineyards has a number of steel barrels to age their wines, such as their Sauvignon Blanc.

This machine is used to label premium wines. Label spools are threaded into the machine, and bottles are placed at the end as the labels are pressed on.

Stainless-steel fermenters face oak barrels waiting to be filled with wine for the aging process at Westbend Vineyards. The bottoms of the fermenters contain pipes that fill the barrels. Grates underneath catch any wayward wine that may spill in the process.

Towering stainless-steel fermenters at Westbend Vineyards await fresh grape juice for fermenting. Some of these machines are used by other local wineries to ferment their wines.

Westbend Vineyards assists other wineries in creating their own wines, so they have different names stamped on the side of their barrels, such as Allison Oaks Vineyards.

cause. More than likely it is because of bacterial contamination, which may clear in a year. Or you may have other options that you can try before just dumping the batch.

You could try using cold to clear it by dropping the temperature of the wine by 10 degrees F. If your wine was 8 degrees F or more to begin with, you may need to drop the temperature by 20 degrees. Try to keep it at this lower temperature for three or more weeks and see if that helps the cloudy haze.

You can also try to add clear wine to it at a ratio of 1:4, or 1 quart of clear wine to every gallon of cloudy wine. You can resort to filtering, but as mentioned earlier in this book, a filter can negatively affect the color and taste of your wine. If you are desperate and have tried everything else to remove the haze, filtering may be your only option. If you do decide to use a filter, you are better off using one with a pump, as gravity-fed filters take a long time and do not always work. They allow the wine to be exposed to oxygen, which can lead to oxidation of the wine.

Bad bacteria can cause some haziness. If you notice a bad odor or taste, it may be time to dump your wine. Make sure you sterilize your equipment thoroughly before starting again. If you see a vinegar mother form on your wine, you may need to buy a new fermenter, as this may spoil future batches of your wine. Sometimes it is malolactic bacteria that can cause haziness, so be careful before adding these to a wine during secondary fermentation. You can tell this is what has happened to your wine if there is a silky sheen to your wine. You can fix this by adding three Campden tablets per gallon of wine. Wait about ten days before racking your wine again.

If you are finding that the finings are not working, make sure you are stirring the must vigorously. This is very important to dissolve and disperse the fining agents. Sometimes CO_2 bubbles will float the fining agents to the top of the fermenter. Stir the must until you do not see any more foam or fizzing.

NO. 6 — MY WINE BECAME CLOUDY IN THE BOTTLE

If your wine was clear before you bottled it and became cloudy after you bottled it, this can mean that fermentation was not complete. Take a sample of your wine and check the SG. If it is higher than the kit instructions or recipe stated it should be, your wine may not be finished. Dump the wine back into the fermenter and allow it to finish fermenting.

NO. 7 — MY WINE IS TOO SWEET

An overly sweet wine is a matter of taste. There are many dessert wines that have a high amount of residual sugar. If you wanted to make a dry wine but it tastes more like breakfast juice, then this can be a problem. Sometimes your wine can have what is called a stuck fermentation. For whatever reason, the yeast you added is not doing its job. The conditions may not be right, or the yeast may have died off. Sometimes this can happen if you racked your wine too soon. This is a common problem with new winemakers. You can fix this problem in a couple of different ways. You can add more yeast and restart fermentation. This will convert the residual sugar into more alcohol. You should use high alcohol-tolerant yeast, and you may consider creating a yeast starter. You can accomplish this by adding yeast to about a ½ cup of the sweet wine; once it begins to ferment, add another ¼ cup of the sweet wine to the starter. Wait about eight hours and add another ¼ cup of wine. Do this same procedure two more times. Once the yeast starter is fermenting strongly, add it to the batch of wine with a ½ teaspoon of nutrient. Allow this fermentation to continue for a month. You will find that the alcohol content of the wine has increased, but the sweetness had decreased.

"There are many people in North Carolina, or who visit North Carolina, that like the taste of really sweet wines, especially using the native grapes such as Muscat or Muscadine."

— Mark Terry, general manager and winemaker; Westbend Vineyards

The second way you can correct the problem is to blend in a very dry wine to your sweet wine. This can change the flavor, and you will never have a totally dry wine.

One of the best ways to deal with a sweet wine is to prevent the issue from happening in the first place. There are many recipes that you can find in wine books or on the Internet that will create overly sweet wines. Some recipes are written in British Imperial gallons, not U.S. gallons. U.S. gallons are smaller than Imperial ones by about 20 percent. If you do not cut back the sugar in your recipe and make it according to Imperial gallons, you will create a rather sweet wine.

The other aspect to consider is that some recipes call for too much sugar to start with. The yeast cannot handle the overly sweet environment and will die off — thus creating stuck fermentation.

You have a few options to choose from in order to use these recipes but not risk cavities.

1. Reduce the sugar in an Imperial gallon recipe by 20 percent. Multiply the number by 4/5 (0.8) to get your amount.

   For example, suppose it calls for 3 lbs. of sugar for 5 Imperial Gallons of wine. You decide to make 5 U.S. gallons of wine, so you must adjust the sugar.

   3.0 x 0.8 = 2.4 lbs. of sugar

2. Do not add all the sugar at once. Add only half of the sugar at the beginning of fermentation. When you rack your wine for secondary fermentation, add one-fourth of the original amount of sugar. After about a week of the secondary fermentation, add the last one-fourth of the original amount of sugar.

   For example: Your recipe calls for 4 lbs. of sugar in a 5-Imperial gallon recipe.

   Primary fermentation = 2 lbs. of sugar

   Beginning of secondary fermentation = 1 lb. of sugar

   One week after secondary fermentation has begun = 1 lb. of sugar

Sometimes your yeast needs a little boost, such as yeast nutrient. If you do not add the recommended amount of yeast nutrient or use the standard ½ teaspoon of yeast nutrient per gallon, you may find that your yeast died off too quickly.

If you are using juice concentrates or even juice that has been shipped to you, you must take into account that they have been heavily sulfured to prevent premature fermentation or spoilage. This can make it difficult to get a fermentation going. The best way to fix this problem is to put the juice in the primary fermenter. Gently rock it back and forth and allow the juice to slosh back and forth — this is called "rock the baby." This releases the free sulphur ions into the air. The other way to aerate it is to pour the juice back and forth between two fermenter buckets. After you finish aerating, add the yeast nutrient and create a yeast starter, as previously mentioned.

Be careful about how much sugar the recipe is telling you to use. Just because you found it on the Internet or even a book does not mean that the recipe is a good one. So if a recipe calls for more than 2 cups of sugar per gallon of wine, be wary; this may be too sweet for the average yeast to deal with.

NO. 8 — MY YEAST SEEMS TIRED

Sometimes weak or slow yeast can slow fermentation. If this happens after you have pitched the yeast, recheck your specific gravity reading. If the reading is less than your original gravity reading, then fermentation is taking place; however, it may be quiet and hidden. Do not worry as long as fermentation is continuing. Check the gravity in a day or two, and make sure that it is still fermenting.

Sometimes the must is too hot for the yeast to work. If the temperature of the must is above 90 degrees F when you pitch the yeast, you may have killed it. You will need to cool down the must and pitch again. You want to get fermentation started as quickly as possible to prevent spoilage. Here are some ideas for cooling your must:

- Wrap your fermenter in a wet T-shirt and turn on a fan to blow on it

- Freeze water in some plastic bottles, sanitize the bottles, and drop them in the must

- Sanitize plastic zippable bags and fill with ice; drop bags into the must

Once the must has reached the desired temperature, you can then pitch some fresh yeast. Always keep some all-purpose wine yeast on hand.

Sometimes you may have the opposite problem, and the must is too cold for the yeast; they might go dormant. Check to see if the temperature is below 65 degrees F. If so, you may need to slightly raise the temperature. You can do this with a blanket of a brew belt. Most yeast will ferment within 24 hours of being pitched. If you find that your yeast does not respond to heat, you may need to add fresh yeast.

NO. 9 — MY WINE HAS A STUCK FERMENTATION

In a wine that is too sweet, the problem could be that too much sugar has been added to the must. There are some other reasons that fermentation stops. There may not be enough nutrients added to the must. Remember, you should put at least ½ teaspoon per gallon. Another reason for a stuck fermentation could be that there is not enough acid in the must, or it could be that the temperature of the environment that the fermentation is occurring in could be too high, too low, or it could be changing too much.

In order to determine what the potential problem is, you should take some measurements of your must. You can check the sugar level, the acid level, and even the temperature of the wine must. You can adjust the acid level if it is too low by adding some acid blend. If you suspect it is yeast that is slow, you can add some yeast nutrient (½ teaspoon per gallon) or even some yeast energizer (¼ teaspoon per gallon).

You can make a yeast starter; after you add it to the wine, make sure the temperature of the wine is at about 70 degrees F. It might take a few days for fermentation to restart. If it does not, create a yeast starter. Red Star Premier Curvee (sometimes called Prise de Mousse) or Lalvin K1-V1116 (sometimes called Montpellier) are great yeasts to use in order to restart a stuck fermentation.

After a couple of days, the yeast starter should be fermenting, and at that point you can add ½ teaspoon of yeast nutrient along with another ½ cup of your wine must. Allow the yeast starter to sit for another six hours; then, if it is actively fermenting, add the yeast starter gently back to the wine must. Do this slowly so that the starter is sitting on top of the wine must and do not stir it. After another 24 hours you can gently stir it, and after another 24 hours you must stir it again, but this time you can do it more vigorously.

NO. 10 — MY WINE HAS A FUNNY COLOR

Sometimes wines can get a colored haze to them that is caused by elements such as copper, zinc, iron, or aluminum that have come into contact with it through the use of some type of implements or even metal primary fermentation vessels that can add a white, dark, purplish, or brown haze to the wine.

In the case of iron or copper, you can clear this haze by adding two to three drops of citric acid. If you suspect that it was zinc or aluminum that has caused the haze, you can try adding clean eggshells to the wine. You can even try filtering the wine to clear it. Sometimes even filtering will not work; the wine will either have to be dumped, or you will have to live with the haze.

NO. 11 — MY WINE GOT DARK

Sometimes a wine can go dark after being decanted. This is often caused by oxidation and is the result of the wine's not being properly stabilized. This can be fixed by adding two Campden tablets to a 5-to-6 gallon batch. If the wine has already been bottled, then you will need to dump the wine back into the fermenter and add the Campden tablets quickly and return them to the bottles. Try to keep the wine from coming in contact with the air, as this can cause further darkening.

There is another cause of the darkening of wine, and that is contact between the wine and iron. This can be fixed by adding ½ ounce of citric acid to a 5-gallon batch of wine. This works out to be just less than ½ teaspoon citric acid per gallon.

NO. 12 — MY WHITE WINE GOT A WEIRD COLOR

You may notice that your white wine will be slightly misty or have an off-white color to it. This usually can be corrected by adding eggshells to it. Prepare the eggshells by cleaning them and drying them in an oven. This process will make the shells brittle, and you can crush them into small pieces, which are then added to the wine. The shells will sink slowly to the bottom over time and will collect carbon dioxide gas that is trapped in the wine. Once this happens, the shells will rise to the surface and release the gas, then begin to sink again. This process of floating and sinking may go on for awhile. As the shells move through the wine, they will collect the chemicals that are causing the off colors and drag them to the bottom of the fermenter.

NO. 13 — MY WINE SMELLS LIKE A MOLDY NEWSPAPER

This is the sign of cork taint that can occur with the use of natural corks. This cork taint is caused by the chemical 2,4,6-trichloro-anisole (TCA) and can sometimes by described as smelling like dirt, wet dog, damp cloth, damp basement, or mushrooms. Many times, if there is a strong cork taint, the wine is not harmful — but it is undrinkable. Airborne fungi, which come in contact with chlorophenol compounds, can cause cork taint. These chemicals are used in pesticides and eventually turn into chloroanisole. Sometimes cork taint can occur if you sterilize your corks in chlorine. Most of the time, there is nothing you can do; your wine is ruined. You can try pouring your wine into a bowl lined with plastic wrap. The theory is that the TCA particles are attracted to the polyethylene in the plastic wrap and hence remove the cork taint. Cork taint will not hurt or kill you; most people would just dump it after smelling the wine, as it is recommended.

NO. 14 — THERE IS A FINGERNAIL-POLISH REMOVER SMELL

The odor of polish remover is the sign of ethyl acetate contamination. This happens one of three ways. The first is when ethyl alcohol and oxygen react to one another. This can produce acetaldehyde, and this in turn can mix with oxygen again and produce acetic acid or vinegar. This vinegar then will react with the residual ethyl alcohol and produce ethyl acetate. The most logical way to stop this process is to reduce the wine's exposure to oxygen during the fermentation process. This can be difficult, so some winemakers will add an inert gas to the top of the wine such as argon, NO or CO_2. This pushes the oxygen out of the vessel before racking.

The second way ethyl acetate contamination can occur is when acetobacter bacteria contaminate the wine. This is because acebactor produces acetic acid, which then reacts to the ethyl alcohol and creates ethyl acetate. The way to prevent this from happening is to maintain a high enough level of sulfur dioxide to prevent the acetobacter from growing.

The third and final way of ethyl acetate contamination occurring is when the yeast is under too much stress. They can produce acetate if the proper temperature is not maintained; the wrong water is used; too much yeast nutrient is used in a country-style wine; or not enough nitrogen was present for some strains of yeast that require it.

One of the ways to deal with ethyl acetate is to run an aquarium pump and attach it to an air stone that is submerged in the wine. The bubbles will disperse the ethyl acetate in a few days. This treatment does hasten oxidation of the wine, so you will need to drink it quickly. Even if the ethyl acetate is removed by the air stone, there may be acetic acid that remains. If this is the case, you will need to dump the wine and sterilize all of your equipment.

NO. 15 — MY WINE IS VERY BITTER

One of the main causes of bitter wine is a contamination called mannite. This wine disease is caused by a bacteria, d-mannite (sometimes called mannitic bacteria or mannite), and occurs when lactic acid bacteria works on sugars. This situation occurs when there is not enough acid in the wine, or when too much heat is created during secondary or malolactic fermentation. This wine disease can be avoided by using sulfur dioxide and making sure the must is cooled after alcoholic fermentation. If the wine has a severe case of mannite, then the wine will be undrinkable.

NO. 16 — MY WINE TASTES OR SMELLS MEDICINAL

This common problem with wine can be the cause of not enough acid in the wine. Make sure that your wine has sufficient acid, and make a note of the problem in your recipe. The next time you make a particular type of wine, the same problem will not happen again.

There can be other reasons for medicinal odors in a wine, such as the production of compounds by the yeast *Brettanomyces bruxellensis* (referred to as "Brett" by many winemakers) and another similar yeast, *Dekkera bruxellensis.* If the medicinal smell is not too strong, you might have a chance to treat the problem. You can add potassium metabisulfite to the wine to raise the level of sulfur dioxide. This will stop the reproduction of Brett in your wine. Another thing you can try is to add activated charcoal to the wine and strain it out after three to eight weeks. If the medicinal smell is strong or the measures did not work, you will have no choice but to dump the wine.

NO. 17 — MY WINE TASTES LIKE TIN

If you use canned fruits in your wine to flavor the wine or to use as the base of your wine, sometimes the fruit can react with the can. This occurs when the acid in the fruit reacts with the metal in the can. If this occurs, there is no cure. Pour out your wine and just be sure to avoid that brand of canned fruit in future batches.

NO. 18 — MY WINE HAS A MOLDY OR MUSTY FLAVOR

Sometimes a moldy off-flavor can occur because you have left your wine on the lees too long without racking it. The lees begin to break down and can leave this type of taste. Also make sure you never use baker's yeast to ferment wine because this can also leave a moldy or musty flavor like old bread. You can treat this condition by adding a Campden tablet and ½ ounce of activated charcoal per gallon of wine. Stir the wine vigorously for a minute or two, then allow it to sit for about six hours. Repeat this procedure about five times, and allow the wine to rest for a day. Pour the wine through cheesecloth; this should cure the off-flavor. You can purchase activated charcoal at a pharmacy or a fish tank supply store.

NO. 19 — MY WINE SMELLS LIKE ROTTEN EGGS

This is caused by hydrogen sulfide and usually occurs at the end of fermentation. Though it will not make your sick, the wine will be undrinkable. There could be a number reasons for this, such as contamination, too many sulfites, or not enough nutrients for the yeast. The earlier you catch the problem, the more likely it will be that you can fix it before you have to dump the wine.

Some people will recommend copper sulfate, but this is poisonous. Instead, rack your wine and aerate it as you go. You can hold the tubing above the fermenter rather than place it inside the fermenter as you are siphoning it. This allows the wine to be exposed to the air before it hits the fermenter. Oxygen will help counteract the effects of hydrogen sulfide. You can pour the wine over copper wire to counteract it as well. Fining agents and filtration can also remove some of the smell. I recommend egg-white or gelatin-fining agents.

NO. 20 — MY WHITE WINE TASTES LIKE VINEGAR

The reason that wine can have a vinegar or Sherry flavor can be from oxidation. It can also be because the wine has been contaminated and has become vinegar. You have two choices: Dump the wine, or save the vinegar and reduce it to create a homemade balsamic. Adding figs or herbs will add interest and create vinegar with sweet, complex flavors that make it a great choice for marinades and salads. Either way, discard the fermentation vessel and make sure you sanitize the rest of your equipment very well before using it again.

NO. 21 — MY WINE TASTES OR SMELLS LIKE PLASTIC

Using the wrong type of container in primary fermentation is the most likely reason for a plastic taste or smell. You should use only food-grade plastic (that is why they make it). Do not use kitchen trash bins or wastebaskets to make your wine.

NO. 22 — MY WINE SMELLS LIKE GERANIUMS

This is caused by an infection of the wine by certain strains of lactic acid bacteria. If a wine has sufficient sorbic acid in it, the bacteria will consume it and produce a substance (2-ethoxyhexa-3,5-diene) that causes the smell. If your wine has this smell, there is no hope; it is destined for the sewer.

NO. 23 — THERE IS AN OIL SLICK IN MY WINE

Wine can appear to have an oily substance floating on top. It can have rope-like threads or strings when you pour the wine, and may move slowly and thickly and have the consistency of egg whites. The smell and taste are not affected. This oil slick is often caused by lactic acid bacterium. The good news is that it is treatable but must be done so immediately, or it can destroy a wine.

The cure is to pour your affected wine in a wide-mouthed container with extra room. You should use an egg beater to whip the wine into a froth. Once it is frothy, add two crushed Campden tablets for every 1 gallon of wine, and stir them in with the egg beater.

After you have stirred it for at least five minutes, cover the container with a sterile cloth. For the next four hours, stir the wine again for five minutes on the hour (a total of four times). After the four hours, return the wine to a secondary fermenter and seal it with an airlock. Allow the wine to sit for two days and then run it through a wine filter and return to a sterile secondary vessel.

NO. 24 — THERE ARE WHITE FLOWERS IN MY WINE

Sometimes you might see small white flecks or white powder on the top of your wine. These may grow if you do not intervene. This infection can cover the top of your wine and grow into a thick white crust. This white bloom is caused by wild yeasts and sometimes by mycoderma bacteria. If you do not do act immediately upon seeing it, then it will quickly spoil your wine.

If the bloom is caused by yeast, this yeast will consume the alcohol in your wine and turn it into nothing but ill-tasting colored water. In order to stop this, you must treat it with potassium metabisulfite at the rate of one Campden tablet per gallon. If you stopped it in time, you may notice some loss of alcohol. You can blend the wine with a higher alcohol wine and consume it quickly.

If mycoderma bacteria caused the bloom, the treatment is about the same: one Campden tablet per gallon of wine. The difference is that bacteria will usually ruin the wine permanently, and it will have to be dumped. Allow your palate to make the decision.

There is an exception to flowers in wine being bad, and that is the use of flor Sherry yeast. In this case, it can be hard to tell if the flower bloom is natural or the cause for concern. The best way to be sure is to properly sulfite your wine.

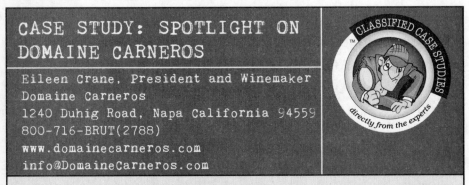

CASE STUDY: SPOTLIGHT ON DOMAINE CARNEROS

Eileen Crane, President and Winemaker
Domaine Carneros
1240 Duhig Road, Napa California 94559
800-716-BRUT(2788)
www.domainecarneros.com
info@DomaineCarneros.com

When Eileen Crane was 8 years old, her father let her taste wine at Sunday dinners and taught her to appreciate the varieties. Crane's father would tell her stories about the different bottles in their wine cellar, and she developed a lifelong love for it.

Throughout college, Crane continued her love for wine; it was a part of her life. She remembers picking out wines for her friends. She lived in Venezuela and worked as a social worker and eventually made her way back to the University of Connecticut to complete her graduate work in nutrition. After she worked as a teacher for a few years, she enrolled in the Culinary Institute of America's ten-week program. It was while completing her work that she heard the University of California at Davis was offering viticulture and enology classes. She talked to the professors at the program and decided that while she did not need another degree, she did want to learn about winemaking.

Crane took classes as UC Davis and found a job as a tour guide at Domaine Chandon, a winery known for its sparkling wines. She quickly moved to working in the pastry kitchen due to her coursework at the CIA, and she then began working in the winery lab.

Crane was hired not only to work as the winemaker at the Gloria Ferrer Winery, but also to be in charge of its construction. Gloria Ferrer gave her further experience in crafting sparkling wines. It was natural that when the Taittinger family and the Kobrand Corporation wanted to build a winery, they asked Crane to help them — and Domaine Carneros was born.

Crane is now the president and winemaker of Domaine Carneros and is making about 45,000 cases of sparkling wines, Chardonnay, and Pinot Noir. Domaine Carneros has one of the largest wine cellars in the world.

Crane strives to make a great sparkling wine that can deliver for the price: about $26. They produce some of the best sparkling wine in the world while practicing organic farming procedures. In spring 2008, Domaine Carneros was certified organic by the California Certified Organic Farmers (CCOF). This was the result of a three-year certification process, but Domaine Carneros has been practicing organic farming since the late 1980s. They were the first organic sparkling winery in the United States.

The winery never used insecticides on the estate and switched to organic substitutes for fertilizers. With this switch, they purchased new equipment to control the weeds, which eliminated the need of herbicides. Finally, in 2005, the vineyards were totally managed organically. To further their sustainable living practices, in 2003 the winery installed the largest photovoltaic solar collection system used in a winery in the world. Other sustainable living facilities were created with lighting by skylights, night-cooling systems to maintain cellar temperature, and building into the earth for insulation. There are owl boxes placed in all four vineyards as a natural system of rodent management.

CHAPTER 7

Country Wines

Now that you have learned the basics, in this chapter you will learn how to make country wines. These wines use sources of sugar other than grapes. This section will discuss different kinds of fruits and how they can be made into a wine. Some of these will be solely fruits, and some will be blends of fruit and grape or combination of fruits.

Pick fruits and vegetables when they are fresh and in-season. Many of the fruits you can buy year-round at the grocery store may lack flavor and even essential sugars. Buy what is in-season.

It is not the best idea to start a watermelon wine in the dead of winter. Go to farmers' markets, as they will always have fruits and vegetables that are fresh and in-season. Winemaking is about planning ahead — think now about what you want to drink next year.

If you just cannot wait to make that raspberry wine, you can buy frozen berries. This is a good option because they are often flash-frozen just after they are picked; they retain sugars, flavor, and color. Make sure you defrost the fruit before dumping it into a fermenter. The freezing cold fruit can slow down or even stop fermentation. Frozen produce has another advantage. When the juices crystallize in the fruit as it freezes, the crystals are often jagged. These crystals break the cell walls in the fruit or vegetable. This allows juice to flow freely when it is defrosted because it is not trapped inside the fruit. Even if you buy fresh fruit, you may want to freeze it for a few days before using it in a wine.

The following is a list of recipes that use different types of fruits other than grapes as their base. In each recipe, you will notice that "standard winemaking equipment" is listed in the ingredients. *You can find a list of standard winemaking equipment in Chapter 2.*

The first couple of recipes are berry wines. Berries are actually produced by the single ovary of the flower of a plant. The entire wall of the ovary ripens and can be eaten. The seeds of the berry are usually embedded in the flesh of the fruit. There are many types of fruits that are called berries but are not technically berries at all, such as blueberries, cranberries, raspberries, and strawberries. The following is a list of true berries:

- Grape
- Tomato

- Barberry
- Currant
- Elderberry
- Gooseberry
- Honeysuckle
- May apple
- Nannyberry
- Oregon-grape
- Sea buckthorn

Most berries are great to use for wine because they usually contain a lot of sugar and are full of flavor. Berry wines are great to make because you might have some of the bushes growing near your house, or you may have a local farmers' market that sells them seasonally.

"I start by getting the fruit, which needs to be completely ripe. If it isn't, there will be too much acid in the wine. I either grow all my own fruit, or pick wild fruit or berries. With grapes, I pick them and then put them on screens outside in the sun to make sure they are ripe.

In the best wine I ever made, I used grapes that had frozen on the vine. They were so ripe, and freezing seemed to preserve them."

— Richard Schlicht, home winemaker

BERRY AND FRUIT WINES

Blackberry Wine

Yield 1 gallon/ 3.8 L

OG = 1.088 FG = 1.014 ABV = 10%

Original Brix (21.25) - Final Brix (3.00) = 18.25 x 0.55 = 10% ABV

Ingredients:

6 lbs. of blackberries

2 ½ lbs. of granulated sugar

½ tsp. pectic enzyme

Water (enough to make 1 gallon of wine must)

1 packet red wine yeast

Cheesecloth or nylon bag

1-gallon carboy

1 tsp. yeast nutrient

Standard winemaking equipment

Instructions:

1. Wash berries thoroughly in colander.

2. Crush berries in a bowl and place them in a nylon bag or cheesecloth.

3. Transfer bag to primary fermentation vessel.

4. Pour about 7 pints of boiling water over fruit bag. Allow to sit for 48 hours.

5. Gently squeeze the bag and remove. Add sugar and stir well to make sure it is completely dissolved. Stir in pectic enzyme and allow to sit for 24 hours.

6. Pitch yeast and nutrient. Stir every day for five to six days.

7. Pour into carboy and attach airlock.

8. Place wine in a cool, dark place for three months.

9. Rack and allow it to sit for another two months.

10. Rack again and bottle.

11. Allow a year to mature.

Strawberry Wine

You may use cultivated or wild strawberries, or a combination of the two.

Yield 1 gallon/3.8 L
OG = 1.090 FG = 1.014 ABV = 10%
Original Brix (21.75) - Final Brix (3.50) = 18.25 x 0.55 = 10% ABV

Ingredients:

4 to 5 pints of strawberries (fresh but not too overripe)
4 ½ cups granulated sugar
1 tsp. yeast nutrient
1 lemon (juice and rind)
1 Campden tablet
½ tsp. pectic enzyme

1 packet wine yeast
Water (enough to make 1 gallon of wine must)
Standard winemaking equipment
1-gallon carboy
Nylon bag/cheesecloth

Instructions:

1. Crush the berries in bottom of primary fermenter.

2. Add sugar, pectic enzyme, and crushed Campden tablets. Stir well to dissolve sugar.

3. Create a yeast starter by adding yeast to ½ cup to 1 cup of water or orange juice, and 1 teaspoon of sugar. Cover tightly and shake well. Allow to sit 24 hours.

4. Pitch yeast starter to berries. Stir well. Cover loosely and stir several times per day for four days. Break the hard crust that will form on top of berries daily.

5. Squeeze out as much juice as you can from the fruit and rack wine must into a carboy and attach airlock.

6. If you wish for your wine to be dry, then you should allow it to mature for three weeks, rack the wine, and allow it to mature for another four weeks. When the wine is clear and no longer needs racking, then it is ready to bottle.

7. If you wish to create a sweeter wine, then you will allow the wine to mature three weeks and rack it into another carboy. Dissolve ½ cup of sugar in 1 cup of wine. Add

this sweetened cup of wine to the carboy. You will need to repeat this process until wine is clear. Bottle when the wine is ready.

8. Allow wine to mature for two full years from the date it was started.

"The amount of fruit you use makes different wine. I use about 2 quarts of fruit per gallon, which makes a nice heavy, wine. The fruit should be as ripe as possible."

— Richard Schlicht, home winemaker

Cranberry Wine

Yield 1 gallon/3.8 L
OG = 1.090 FG = 1.014 ABV = 10%
Original Brix (21.75) - Final Brix (3.50) = 18.25 x 0.55 = 10% ABV

Ingredients:

2 lbs. cranberries, fresh or frozen
1 lb. raisins
3 lbs. granulated sugar (about 6 ¾ cups)
1 Campden tablet
1 tsp. nutrients
¼ tsp. pectic enzyme
1 ¼ tsp. acid blend
Standard winemaking equipment
1-gallon carboy
Water (enough to make 1 gallon of wine must)

1 crushed Campden tablet

1 packet wine yeast

Instructions:

1. Place fruit into cheesecloth/bag. Place in primary fermenter and crush the fruit. Transfer the berry bag to your fermentation bucket.

2. Pour a gallon of boiling water over fruit bag. Allow to sit for 48 hours.

3. Gently squeeze the bag and remove. Add sugar and stir well to make sure it is completely dissolved. Add pectic enzyme, cover well, and allow it to sit for 24 hours.

4. Add yeast, energizer, and tannin; cover and set aside five to six days, stirring daily.

5. Pour into carboy and attach airlock.

6. If you wish for your wine to be dry, then you should allow it to mature for three weeks, rack the wine and then allow it to mature for another four weeks. When the wine is clear and no longer needs racking, then it is ready to bottle.

7. If you wish to create a sweeter wine, then you will allow the wine to mature three weeks and then rack it into another carboy. Dissolve ½ cup sugar in a 1 cup of wine. Add this sweetened cup of wine to the carboy. You will need to repeat this process until wine is clear. Bottle when the wine is ready.

8. Mature wine a year from the date it was started.

Blueberry Wine

Yield 1 gallon/3.8 L

OG = 1.09 FG = 1.014 ABV = 10%

Original Brix (21.75) - Final Brix (3.50) = 18.25 x 0.55 = 10% ABV

Ingredients:

2 ½ lbs. blueberries (any variety)

1 lb. raisins

2 lbs. granulated sugar

½ tsp. pectic enzyme

1½ tsp. acid blend

½ tsp. yeast energizer

Standard winemaking equipment

1 gallon carboy

Water (enough to make 1 gallon of wine must)

1 crushed Campden tablet

1 packet wine yeast

Instructions:

1. Place fruit into cheesecloth/bag. Place in primary fermenter and crush the fruit. Transfer the berry bag to your fermentation bucket.

2. Pour a gallon of boiling water over fruit bag. Allow to sit for 48 hours.

3. Gently squeeze the bag and remove. Add sugar and stir well to make sure it is completely dissolved. Add pectic enzyme, cover well, and allow it to sit for 24 hours.

4. Add yeast, energizer, and tannin; cover and set aside five to six days, stirring daily.

5. Pour into carboy and attach airlock.

6. If you want your wine to be dry, then you should allow it to mature for three weeks, rack the wine, then allow it to mature for another four weeks. When the wine is clear and no longer needs racking, then it is ready to bottle.

7. If you wish to create a sweeter wine, then you will allow the wine to mature three weeks and then rack it into another carboy. Dissolve ½ cup sugar in a 1 cup of wine. Add this sweetened cup of wine to the carboy. You will need to repeat this process until wine is clear. Bottle when the wine is ready.

8. Mature wine a year from the date it was started.

The next types of country wines you can make are pitted fruit wines. These types of fruits have one large pit in them instead of many smaller seeds. These fruits also have distinct flavors and a good amount of sugar, which make them excellent candidates to be included in wine. The pits should always be removed when making a wine. These pits contain small amounts of cyanide. Although a person would have to consume a great number of pits to be poisoned, why take the chance? Often these pits can leave off-flavors in wine. The easiest way to remove a pit, or stone, is to slice the fruit in half, then pull the pit out.

Sometimes you can blanch the fruit. This is a quick boil that loosens the skin so that it can be removed from the pulp inside. Freezing the pulp can help you extract more juice from it.

Never use canned fruits, as these contain sugar in the form of corn syrup, which does not work well in wines. They also contain preservatives that will make fermentation almost impossible.

Peach Wine

Yield 1 gallon/3.8 L
OG = 1.09 FG = 1.014 ABV = 10%
Original Brix (21.75) - Final Brix (3.50) = 18.25 x 0.55 = 10% ABV

Ingredients:

2 ½ to 3 lbs. peaches (very ripe)
2 lbs. white sugar
1 lb. dark brown sugar
1 tsp. acid blend
¼ tsp. grape tannin
¾ tsp. pectic enzyme
1 tsp. yeast nutrient
1 packet of yeast (Lalvin 71B-1122 is preferred for this recipe)
Standard winemaking equipment
Nylon bag or cheesecloth
1-gallon carboy

Instructions:

1. Remove stones from the peaches and chop fruit. Place in bag or cloth. Add water, sugar, Campden tablet, and bag to primary fermenter. Stir to dissolve sugar. Let sit 24 hours. Add nutrients, tannin, and pectic enzyme. Make

sure the OG is between 1.090 and 1.095 (Brix = 22.0 to 22.5). Pitch yeast. Stir daily for three days.

2. Take out bag and gently squeeze out juice. Rack into carboy fermenter and attach airlock.

3. If you wish for your wine to be dry, then you should allow it to mature for three weeks, rack the wine, then allow it to mature for another four weeks. When the wine is clear and no longer needs racking, then it is ready to bottle.

4. If you wish to create a sweeter wine, then you will allow the wine to mature three weeks; then, rack it into another carboy. Dissolve ½ cup of sugar in 1 cup of wine. Add this sweetened cup of wine to the carboy. You will need to repeat this process until wine is clear. Bottle when the wine is ready.

5. Mature wine for one full year from the date it was started.

Apricot Wine

Yield 1 gallon/3.8 L
OG = 1.040 FG = 1.014 ABV = 10%
Original Brix (21.75) - Final Brix (3.50) = 18.25 x 0.55 = 10% ABV

Ingredients:

3 lbs. whole ripe, firm apricots
2 1bs. sugar
1 ½ tsp. acid blend
5 drops liquid pectic enzyme

¼ tsp. tannin

Hot water (enough to make 1 gallon of wine must)

½ tsp. yeast energizer

1 tablet Campden tablets

1 packet of wine yeast (try Cote des Blancs or Lalvin 71B-1122)

Cheesecloth or nylon bag

Standard winemaking equipment

1-gallon carboy

Instructions:

1. Place apricots in fruit bag or cheesecloth and place in primary fermenter.

2. Add hot water, sugar, nutrients, acid, pectic enzyme, tannin, and Campden tablet. Make sure to stir and dissolve sugar. Let it sit 24 hours.

3. Specific gravity should be 1.090 to 1.095 (Brix = 22.0 to 22.5). Stir in yeast. Stir daily for five to six days or until specific gravity is 1.040 (Brix = 3.5).

4. Gently squeeze bag. Throw away the fruit or add to your compost. Rack into carboy and add airlock.

5. If you wish to have dry wine, rack in three weeks and again in four weeks. Continue racking every month until wine is clear. Bottle.

6. If you wish to have sweet wine, rack at three weeks. Add ½ cup sugar dissolved in 1 cup wine. Stir and place back into carboy. Repeat process every six weeks until specific gravity is stable. Rack in three weeks, and again in four

weeks. Continue racking every month until wine is clear. Bottle when the wine is ready.

7. Mature the wine a year from the date you began the process.

Cherry Wine

Yield 1 gallon/3.8 L
OG = 1.09 FG = 1.014 ABV = 10%
Original Brix (21.75) - Final Brix (3.50) = 18.25 x 0.55 = 10% ABV

Ingredients:

38 lbs. cherries (choose your favorite variety)
3 ½ lbs. sugar
Water (enough to make 1 gallon of wine must)
3 tsp. pectic enzyme
3 Campden tablets
½ tsp. tannin
1 packet Premier cuvee yeast
Standard winemaking equipment
Nylon bag or cheesecloth
1-gallon carboy

Instructions:

1. De-stem cherries and take out pits by hand. If you have a pitter, this job will be easier. You can also stomp on the cherries like grapes.

2. Place cherries in bag or cheesecloth. Hold over fermenter and crush cherries. Place cherry bag in the primary fermenter.

3. Boil the remainder of the water and dissolve the sugar. Allow the water to cool and cover the fruit with the sugar water. Stir in pectic enzyme and Campden tablets. Allow to sit for 48 hours.

4. Gently squeeze bag to get as much juice as possible. Add the rest of the ingredients except yeast. Make sure that the level of liquid is 1 gallon by adding water. Make sure SG is between 1.070 and 1.110 (17 to 24 Brix). Pitch yeast and mix in well. Stir must for five days or until rapid fermentation ceases.

5. If you want your wine to be dry, then you should allow it to mature for three weeks, rack the wine, and allow it to mature for another four weeks. When the wine is clear and no longer needs racking, then it is ready to bottle.

6. If you wish to create a sweeter wine, then you will allow the wine to mature three weeks and then rack it into another carboy. Dissolve ½ cup of sugar in 1 cup of wine. Add this sweetened cup of wine to the carboy. You will need to repeat this process until wine is clear. Bottle when the wine is ready.

7. Allow to mature a year.

Plum Wine

Yield 1 gallon/3.8 L
OG = 1.100 FG = 1.040 ABV = 10%
Original Brix (24.00) - Final Brix (5.75) = 18.25 x 0.55 = 10% ABV

Ingredients:

5 lbs. fully ripened plums

Water (enough to make 1 gallon of wine must)

2 ½ lbs. of sugar or honey

1 ½ tsp. of acid blend

⅛ tsp. of tannin

1 tsp. yeast nutrient

Pectic enzyme

1 packet of yeast (Champagne or Montracet is recommended.
You may use sweet mead yeast, especially if you are
using honey)

1 Campden tablet, crushed and dissolved

Fining agent per manufacturer's instructions

Standard winemaking equipment

1-gallon carboy

Nylon bag or cheesecloth

Instructions:

1. Cut plums in half and remove the pits. Leave the skins.
    Crush the fruits by hand. Some plums can be hard, so
    you can put them in a fruit grinder, if you have one.
    Squeeze the juice out of the plums, and place the plums
    in the bag or cheesecloth. Place bag in the fermenter.
    Boil a ½ gallon of water and dissolve the sugar in it by
    stirring. If you are using honey, then skim any foam that
    forms on the top. Add ½ gallon of water and sugar to the
    fermentation bucket. Allow the liquid to cool to room
    temperature, and then add tannin, yeast nutrient, and the
    Campden tablet.

2. Your total acid test should read about 0.65 to 0.75. If it is already at this level, you will not need to add any additional acid blend. If it is lower, than you should add the acid blend. If the total acidity is too high, you can add some water and sugar to adjust the acidity. Try to avoid dilution if possible. Allow the fermenter to sit for 12 hours. Add pectic enzyme according to manufacturer's instructions. Allow must to sit another 24 hours.

3. Take a sanitized smasher and crush the fruit. I have found that a potato masher is great to use. Pitch the yeast.

4. Stir daily until the standard gravity reaches 1.040 (10 Brix), or the active fermentation has ceased. Remove the bag and gently squeeze out the juice. Discard the remaining fruit pulp.

5. Allow the wine to settle in another week. Rack to the secondary fermenter. You may wish to add a Campden tablet.

6. After two weeks, rack again. Add water to raise the level back to 1 gallon. You may add a Campden tablet.

7. Allow to sit for another two to six months. You may want to rack the wine monthly.

8. Once the wine has begun to clear and the SG levels are stabilized, you may add a stabilizer and clarifier.

9. I have found that plum wine is best a little sweetened. You may add about 2 to 6 ounces of sugar in a little water to taste.

10. When you are sure the wine has stabilized, you may bottle it. Allow wine to mature from six to 12 months. This wine improves greatly with age.

I earned my first wine competition prize with this recipe, at the North Carolina State Fair. I had bought a number of juicy plums at the local market and at the grocery store. I took them home, cut and removed the stones, then squeezed each plum by hand. I sent two bottles to Raleigh for the state fair wine competition, and later received a letter and a check in the mail; I was the winner of the first place in the non-grape wine competition. I was so excited, and it only added to my obsession to create more wine at home. I have recreated this wine many years since, but none of them quite match the sweet taste of victory like the wine I made that first year.

There is no technical group of fruits called seeded fruits, but I organized them according to fruits that have many seeds in them. Some of these come from trees and others from vines. Most of these require you to remove the seeds before they are used in a wine. Many times this is done by hand. If the seeds are small and intact, they may be used in a wine and discarded when the wine is racked. The important thing is that you do not break the seeds, so that off-flavors do not seep into the wine.

Kiwi Wine

Yield 1 gallon/3.8 L
OG = 1.100 FG = 1.014 ABV = 10%
Original Brix (24.00) - Final Brix (5.75) = 18.25 x 0.55 = 10% ABV

Ingredients:

3 pints chopped kiwi fruits
½ lb. raisins
2 ½ lbs. granulated sugar
Juice of two oranges
1 tsp. pectic enzyme
Wine yeast
1 tsp. yeast nutrient
1 Campden tablet
Water (enough to make 1 gallon of wine must)
1 packet wine yeast
Standard winemaking equipment
1-gallon carboy

Instructions:

1. Put all of the ingredients in the primary fermenter except the yeast. Make sure the liquid reaches 1 gallon by adding cold water. Let sit 24 hours.

2. Pitch yeast. Leave for five days, stirring daily until rapid fermentation ceases.

3. Rack into carboy. Top off with water. Attach airlock.

4. Rack after three weeks. Return wine to carboy.

5. If you want your wine to be dry, then you should allow it to mature for three weeks, rack the wine, then allow it to mature for another four weeks. When the wine is clear and no longer needs racking, then it is ready to bottle.

6. If you wish to create a sweeter wine, then you will allow the wine to mature three weeks and will rack it into another carboy. Dissolve ½ cup of sugar in 1 cup of wine. Add this sweetened cup of wine to the carboy. You will need to repeat this process until wine is clear. Bottle when the wine is ready.

7. Allow to mature a year.

Melon Wine

Yield 1 gallon/3.8 L
OG = 1.100 FG = 1.014 ABV = 10%
Original Brix (24.00) - Final Brix (5.75) = 18.25 x 0.55 = 10% ABV

Ingredients:

4 pints melon juice (One medium or large melon of your choice. For smaller melons, you may need more)
⅛ tsp. tannin (or cup of black tea)
2 lbs. granulated sugar
2 ½ tsp. acid blend
Wine yeast
1 tsp. yeast nutrient
Water (enough to make 1 gallon of wine must)
1 Campden tablet
1 tsp. pectic enzyme
1-gallon carboy
Standard winemaking equipment
Nylon bag or cheesecloth

Instructions:

1. Cut and scoop out the flesh of the melon. Add to the bag or cloth and squeeze out the juice into the fermenter. Add crushed Campden tablets, sugar, nutrients, and bag to fermenter. Pour 1 quart of boiling water over fruit bag. Cover and let sit 24 hours.

2. Make sure the SG is about 1.100 (24 Brix). Add pectic enzyme and pitch the yeast. Stir daily for five days.

3. Remove bag, and strain and rack liquid to put into carboy. Add water to make up to 1 gallon. Attach an airlock.

4. If you wish for your wine to be dry, then you should allow it to mature for three weeks, rack the wine, and then allow it to mature for another four weeks. When the wine is clear and no longer needs racking, then it is ready to bottle.

5. If you wish to create a sweeter wine, then you will allow the wine to mature three weeks and rack it into another carboy. Dissolve ½ cup of sugar in 1 cup of wine. Add this sweetened cup of wine to the carboy. You will need to repeat this process until wine is clear. Bottle when the wine is ready.

6. Mature wine for a year and a half from the date it was started.

I grew up in Florida with orange, grapefruit, and tangerine trees in my backyard. I loved picking the fruit straight from the tree. There was nothing to compare to fresh fruit juice directly from the source.

Orange Wine

Yield 1 gallon/3.8 L
OG = 1.010 FG = 1.001 ABV = 10%

Ingredients:

12 oranges

2 lemons

3 ½ lbs. sugar

Pectic enzyme

Water (enough to make 1 gallon of wine must)

Yeast nutrient

Wine yeast

½ tsp. pectic enzyme

⅛ tsp. tannin

1 crushed Campden tablet

Wine yeast

½ tsp. potassium sorbate

Standard winemaking equipment

Instructions:

1. Juice all the oranges and lemons. Be careful not to get seeds or peel in the juice. Save a peel and juiced pulp from one of the grapefruit. Clean out the pith from the inside of the peel and add it to the juice along with half of

the sugar, the Campden tablet, tannin, yeast nutrient, and water to make 1 gallon of juice.

2. Dissolve the sugar well in the mixture by stirring. Add the pulp. Allow the juice to sit 12 to 18 hours covered.

3. Add the pectic enzyme per manufacturer's instructions. Allow the juice to sit for at least 12 more hours.

4. Pitch the yeast. After two days of fermentation, add the remaining sugar and dissolve it well. Allow another four to five days of fermentation.

5. Strain out the peel and pulp through a strainer and rack into carboy.

6. For dry wine, rack in three weeks, and again in four weeks. Continue racking every month until wine is clear. Bottle when the wine is ready.

7. For sweet wine, rack at three weeks. Add ½ cup of sugar dissolved in 1 cup of wine. Stir gently, and place back into carboy. Repeat process every six weeks until specific gravity is stable. Rack every month until wine is clear. Bottle when the wine is ready.

8. Allow wine to mature for at least six months.

VEGETABLE WINES

As we move from fruits to vegetables, you may be skeptical whether these types of wines will taste good. However, vegetables come from plants just like fruits do, and they contain natural sugars, also just like fruits. They do not contain as much sugar as many fruits do, so you will add more sugar. This is not only to balance the taste, but also to bring up the potential alcohol content of your wine. Give these vegetable wines a chance; their flavors can be subtle but delicious.

Potato Wine

Yield 1 gallon/ 3.8 L
OG = 1.100 FG = 1.014 ABV = 10%
Original Brix (24.00) - Final Brix (5.75) = 18.25 x 0.55 = 10% ABV

Ingredients:

2 ½ lbs. white potatoes
1 lb. pearl barley
3 lbs. sugar
½ lb. chopped sultanas
2 oranges
1 Campden tablet
Water (enough to make 1 gallon of wine must)
1 packet wine yeast
Standard winemaking equipment
1-gallon carboy
Nylon bag or cheesecloth

Instructions:

1. Bring water to a boil. Clean and scrub the outside of the potatoes. Dice them and place in bag or cloth along with sultanas and barley. Place bag in primary fermenter. Pour boiling water into fermenter. Add sugar, stirring to dissolve. Let sit 24 hours.

2. Be sure that the specific gravity is between 1.090 (21.75 Brix) and 1.100 (24.00 Brix). Slice the whole orange with the rind and add to primary fermenter. Add the remaining ingredients, including the yeast. For five days, stir once a day for five minutes, as fermentation begins.

3. Remove bag and gently squeeze. Rack into secondary fermenter and attach airlock.

4. If you want your wine to be dry, then you should allow it to mature for three weeks, rack the wine, then allow it to mature for another four weeks. When the wine is clear and no longer needs racking, then it is ready to bottle.

5. For a sweet wine, rack at three weeks. Add ½ cup of sugar dissolved in 1 cup of wine. Stir gently, and place back into carboy. Repeat process every six weeks until specific gravity is stable. Rack every month until wine is clear. Bottle when the wine is ready.

6. Mature the wine for one full year from the date it was started.

Carrot Wine

Yield 1 gallon/ 3.8 L
OG = 1.090 FG = 1.014 ABV = 10%
Original Brix (21.75) - Final Brix (3.50) = 18.25 x 0.55 = 10% ABV

Ingredients:

3 ½ lbs. carrots
1 lb. raisins

5 cups granulated sugar

½ tsp. yeast energizer

6 oranges (juice and rind)

¼ tsp. tannin

1 Campden tablet

1 packet wine yeast

Water (enough to make 1 gallon of wine must)

Standard winemaking equipment

1-gallon carboy

Instructions:

1. Wash and scrub carrots and chop into small pieces. Put them into a pot and boil them for about 15 to 20 minutes until they are soft. Strain the liquid into the primary fermenter. Do not press the carrot mash.

2. Add more water to carrot pieces and boil again for about five minutes. Strain into primary fermenter and, again, do not press the carrots. Discard the carrot mash. Add enough water to the liquid to make 1 gallon.

3. Cut up raisins and add to fermenter. Add the remaining ingredients except the yeast. Let sit 24 hours.

4. Be sure that the SG is 1.090 (21.75 Brix) and 1.100 (24.00 Brix). Pitch yeast. Stir the must once a day for five minutes for three or four days, or until rapid fermentation ceases. Rack the wine in five days, or the orange peel could leave a bitter taste in the wine.

5. Strain and rack into carboy. Attach airlock.

6. If you wish for your wine to be dry, then you should allow it to mature for three weeks, rack the wine, and let it mature for another four weeks.

Parsley Wine

Yield 1 gallon/ 3.8 L

OG = 1.100 FG = 1.014 ABV = 10%

Original Brix (24.00) - Final Brix (5.75) = 18.25 x 0.55 = 10% ABV

Ingredients:

1 lb. parsley

3 Campden tablets

2 oranges

2 lemons

7 cups sugar

Pectic enzyme

Yeast nutrients

1 packet wine yeast

Water (enough to make 1 gallon of wine must)

Standard winemaking equipment

1-gallon carboy

Nylon bag or cheesecloth

Instructions:

1. Wash parsley. Chop parsley and put the pieces in the bag. Wash oranges and lemons. Slice the fruit into thin pieces and add to parsley in the bag. Place bag in the primary fermenter. Add sugar and the nutrients.

2. Pour 1 quart of boiling water over sugar to dissolve. After it cools, add pectic enzyme. Let sit for 24 hours.

3. Be sure the SG is between 1.090 (21.75 Brix) and 1.100 (24.00 Brix). Pitch yeast and stir for five days, until rapid fermentation ceases.

4. Remove the bag and gently squeeze. Rack into the carboy and attach airlock.

5. If you wish for your wine to be dry, then you should allow it to mature for three weeks, rack the wine, then allow it to mature for another four weeks. When the wine is clear and no longer needs racking, then it is ready to bottle.

6. For a sweet wine, rack at three weeks. Add ½ cup of sugar dissolved in 1 cup of wine. Stir gently and place back into carboy. Repeat process every six weeks until specific gravity is stable. Rack every month until wine is clear. Bottle when the wine is ready.

HERB AND PLANT WINES

Most herbs and other plants do not contain enough residual sugar to ferment and therefore require added sugar. The trick with herbs is to know how to draw the volatile oils from them in order to experience their unique flavors.

Before you proceed, be warned about a few things. Unless you know what you are doing, it is not recommended that you pick strange plants and herbs and try to make a wine out of them. Some herbs are poisonous, and there are even plants that look like a particular plant but are, in fact, a totally different plant.

The best way to be sure that you are using the right herb and that it was picked legally is to grow it yourself. Many herbs can be grown in pots or in a simple plot next to your house. If at all possible, do not use pesticides on your herbs or any other plant you are using to create wine. If you do use some sort of herbicide or pesticide, wash the plants thoroughly before using.

The second best way to obtain herbs is to go to local farmers' markets. They will often have vendors that sell different types of fresh and potted herbs. Make sure that you are using fresh herbs and not dried herbs. Each of these recipes requires the use of fresh herbs, and the use of dried herbs can have mixed results. They would have to be used in different amounts, and dried herbs are sometimes treated with chemicals to preserve them. These preservatives can ruin your wine.

If you do choose to pick wild herbs to create wines from them, you should not pick them in populated areas such as roadsides. These herbs can be tainted by all of the exhaust they filter every day. You should instead find a meadow away from populated areas. Be sure that you are not picking plants in a national park because there are laws against this activity.

Oak Leaf Wine

Yield 1 gallon/ 3.8 L
OG = 1.110 FG = 1.014 ABV = 5%
Original Brix (25.75) - Final Brix (16.25) = 9.50 x 0.55 = 5% ABV

Ingredients:

8 pints of young, freshly picked oak tree leaves
Water (enough to make 1 gallon of wine must)

3 lbs. cane sugar or 3 ½ lbs. honey
1 tsp. yeast nutrient
1 tsp. tannin
3 tsp. acid blend
1 Campden tablet
Wine yeast
1-gallon carboy
Standard winemaking equipment

Instructions:

1. Remove any dead leaves, bugs, and debris from the oak leaves. Rinse the leaves in cold water and then place in a 2-quart (2-liter) saucepan with 1 quart of water. Bring oak leaves to a simmer. As soon as it starts simmering, remove the pan from the burner and let sit for one to two hours.

2. Dissolve the sugar in boiling water. Strain the oak leaf solution and infused water to the sugar water. Dissolve the tannin, yeast nutrient, Campden tablet, and 1 tsp. of the acid. Pour mixture into the fermenter. Allow to sit overnight.

3. Take a hydrometer reading. It should be around 1.110 (25.250 Brix). Pitch the yeast.

4. If you want your wine to be dry, then you should allow it to mature for three weeks, rack the wine, then allow it to mature for another four weeks. When the wine is clear and no longer needs racking, then it is ready to bottle.

5. For a sweet wine, rack at three weeks. Add ½ cup of sugar dissolved in 1 cup of wine. Stir gently, and place back into carboy. Repeat process every six weeks until specific gravity is stable. Rack every month until wine is clear. Bottle when the wine is ready.

6. Mature this wine for a year from the date it was started.

Elderflower Wine

Yield 1 gallon/3.8 L
OG = 1.100 FG = 1.014 ABV = 10%
Original Brix (24.0) - Final Brix (6.5) = 17.5 x 0.55 = 9.6% ABV

Ingredients:

1 pint elderflowers (can be purchased from most
winemaking suppliers)
3 lbs. sugar
1 orange
2 lemons
Water (enough to make 1 gallon of wine must)
3 cups raisins
1 packet wine yeast
1-gallon carboy
Nylon bag or cheesecloth
Standard winemaking equipment

Instructions:

1. Remove any dead leaves, bugs, and debris from the flowers. Rinse the flowers in cold water and place in a 2-quart (2-liter) saucepan with 1 quart of water. Bring flowers to a simmer. As soon as it starts simmering,

remove the saucepan from the burner and allow it to sit for one to two hours.

2. Dissolve the sugar in boiling water. Strain the elderflowers and infused water to the sugar water. Add raisins. Cut citrus fruits, squeeze into fermenter, and add to the bag. Pour mixture into the fermenter. Allow to sit overnight.

3. Take a hydrometer reading. It should be around 1.110 (24 Brix). Pitch the yeast.

4. If you want your wine to be dry, then you should allow it to mature for three weeks, rack the wine, then allow it to mature for another four weeks. When the wine is clear and no longer needs racking, it is ready to bottle.

5. For a sweet wine, rack at three weeks. Add ½ cup of sugar dissolved in 1 cup of wine. Stir gently and place back into carboy. Repeat process every six weeks until specific gravity is stable. Rack every month until wine is clear. Bottle when the wine is ready.

6. Mature this wine for a year from the date it was started.

Lemon Thyme Wine

Yield 1 gallon/3.8 L
OG = 1.100 FG = 1.014 ABV = 10%
Original Brix (24.0) - Final Brix (6.5) = 17.5 x 0.55 = 9.6% ABV

Ingredients:

1 pint lemon thyme (do not use the stalks)

2 lbs. raisins

1 cup honey

3 lbs. cane sugar

3 lemons

2 oranges

2 Tbsp. acid blend

1 tsp. nutrients

3 Campden tablets

1 packet wine yeast

Water (enough to make 1 gallon of wine must)

Standard winemaking equipment

1-gallon carboy

Nylon bag or cheesecloth

Instructions:

1. Boil the honey in 4 cups water in a large pot. Skim off the foam that will form. Continue to boil until there is no longer any foam.

2. Dissolve sugar and with a quart of water and bring to a boil. Add nutrients and Campden tablets. Remove mixture from the heat.

3. Add lemon thyme, fruit juices, raisins, and grated rinds into a bag/cloth. Place bag in primary fermenter. Pour boiled sugar mixture over the bag and allow it to sit for 24 hours.

4. Specific gravity should be 1.100 (24 Brix). Add yeast. Stir daily for five days.

5. Remove bag and rack liquid to the carboy. Attach an airlock. Rack when fermentation ceases, which will take about six weeks.

6. For a dry wine, rack in three weeks and again in four weeks. Continue racking every month until wine is clear. Bottle when the wine is ready.

CASE STUDY: SPOTLIGHT ON URRACA WINES

John Langley, Owner
Urraca Wines
Cochabamba 9384
Agrelo, Lujan de Cuyo, 5509
Mendoza, Argentina
www.urracawines.com

CLASSIFIED CASE STUDIES
directly from the experts

If you have ever turned on the television in the past 20 or more years, you may have heard the song lyrics *"Bad boys, bad boys, whatcha gonna do…"* If you remember this theme, then you know John's Langley's television show, *Cops*. He is a writer, producer, and director. In 2005, he started a new venture with his children, Morgan and Zac — winemaking. The name Urraca was a nickname given to Langley by his wife; it means "magpie." He felt that the images of animals and wine sell well together.

Langley's goal is the pursuit of excellence, rather than the pursuit of commerce. He says "Alcohol runs in our blood" when referring to his family's love of wine. His love started 20 years before opening his winery, when his wife introduced him to the great French wine Montrachet. Before tasting that exceptional vintage, he did not give much thought to wine.

Langley is not a huge fan of California wines, so he and his family began the search for the right place. He found that land in the California wine country was very price-prohibitive. So when he found a vineyard in Argentina and tasted their wines, he knew he had found the right place. He bought the land and began the process of making wine. Langley feels that the Andes is the perfect place for a vineyard. The vines pick up everything from their environment, so the fact that the water was unpolluted and the air and soil were clean meant that they would produce a great-tasting wine.

Langley was not looking to build a huge winery; he wanted it to be like a small boutique. He was looking to create a great wine, not necessarily to become rich off the earnings of the vineyard. He had found the perfect place, but he needed the best winemaker in Argentina and sought out Walter Blessia. He eventually got him to agree to craft and create wines for Urraca.

The winery produces about 50,000 bottles a year. They have an even greater capacity but want to keep things small for now. They sell some of their grapes to other wineries in Europe, Mexico, and even the Far East.

CHAPTER 8

Meads

"By making this wine vine known to the public, I have rendered my country as great a service as if I had enabled it to pay back the national debt."

— Thomas Jefferson

M eads are one of the most ancient brews on earth. Legend has it that honey once dripped from a honeycomb into water, and natural yeasts fermented the draught. Then, according to legend, some brave individual drank it. Mead is essentially honey wine. It uses honey as its sugar source, and the type of honey used imparts certain flavors, aroma, and colors to the wine. Bees feeding from different flower sources produce types of honey. For instance, bees in certain parts of Florida and California live or are placed near orange groves. The nectar and pollen are brought back to the hive by the bees. The orange nectar and pollen then becomes part of the honey. It gives a light orange flavor and color, and therefore is referred to as orange blossom honey.

You can experiment and mix and match all different types of honey. Like wine and cider, there are different forms of mead: sweet, dry, still, and sparkling. Mead is also broken up into other specific categories according to what types of ingredients are added to it. Even though mead can stand on its own as a delicious drink, there are many other combinations of ingredients that make this type of wine special.

Norse myths concerning mead:

The Vikings' favorite drink was mead, as they believed that it was sent from the gods themselves. The Vikings believed that when they died in battle, they would ascend to Valhalla, which was a great mead hall for fallen warriors.

According to an ancient myth, there was a wise creature named Kvasir whose knowledge and wisdom were so legendary that the two mighty dwarves, Fiallar and Gallar, became jealous of him. Their envy of Kvasir drove them to kill him in order to steal his wisdom. The dwarves mixed honey with his blood and brewed it into mead, which became known as the "holy mead" or "mead of inspiration." It was believed that anyone who drank this mystical drink would gain wisdom. And if the person was already wise, drinking the mead would give him or her godlike wisdom.

A giant named Gilling accused the dwarves of the murder. The giant's son required the dwarves to deposit their mead into three vessels, which were known as Odhroerir (inspiration), Son (offering), and Boden (expiation). Two guardians, Suttung and his daughter Gunlod, watched over the mead, secured in a mountain hideaway.

Odin's two ravens, called Huginn (thought) and Muninn (memory), reported to Odin what had befallen Kvasir. Odin set off to gather the holy mead and attempted to barter for work with Baugi, who was Suttung's brother, in exchange for access to Gunlod's chamber. Baugi did not want to do this, but he faced losing his harvest. He bored a hole through the rock, which led to Gunlod's chamber. Once inside, Odin was able to seduce Gunlod and, during the process, took sips of the holy mead. However, rather than swallowing it, he held it in his mouth. He drained the contents of all three containers.

Odin escaped with the mead in his mouth and then discharged it into three containers in his home of Asgaard. He hid the mead in a well. The three vessels were named Heiddraupnir (light dropper); Hoddrofnir (treasure opener); and Odhroerir (exciter of the heart). The three vessels belong to the three Norns or Wyrd sisters.

This story demonstrates how important mead was to the Nordic races and that it was sacred in both its creation and when imbibed.

Mike Helton's obstacles to creating wine:

1. Knowledge

I had to learn the vocabulary of winemaking. I had to understand what things meant, so I read all of the books on winemaking that I could get my hands on. I scoured the Internet and joined a e-mail list about wine. I read and I listened and I learned. I looked up the different schools around the nation that taught winemaking. I looked up the classes they offered and bought the books that they used. Some of them were really helpful, while others still sit on my shelf because they are so technical in nature it takes years to absorb. I talked to everyone I could find willing to share their knowledge.

There are certain books that I reread every year in accordance to the particular season that I find myself in. There are always ideas that pop out that I had either forgotten or had missed in previous readings.

2. I did not want to embarrass myself

When I first began making wine, I was terrified that I was going to create a horrible wine that would be an embarrassment to those who had taught me how to make wine. I wanted to duplicate the things that worked and increase the quality of the wine I produce. I learned things as I went along. I really enjoyed cooking prior to winemaking, which taught me that I have a sensitive palate, and I have learned to trust my ability to taste my wines and judge their quality. Over time, this fear of embarrassment has lessened — but not my quest to always improve the wines that we produce.

— Mike Helton, vintner; Hanover Park Winery

KING MIDAS GOLDEN ELIXIR

Many people have heard the legend of King Midas, who turned everything he touched into gold. While there was a legendary King Midas, there was an actual historical one as well. He was a ruler of the Phrygian Empire in the area of the world that is now known as Turkey. His final resting place is a large funeral mound that was discovered in 1957 by noted archeologist Rodney Young. This site was dated about 718 BCE and contained a number of pots and furniture. Many of the materials were from his final funeral feast. This could have been the end of the story, as in 1957, the ability to analyze materials was not as advanced as they are today. The pots and other materials were cataloged, bagged, and sent to the University of Pennsylvania.

Fast-forward 40 years into the future. This is when Dr. Patrick McGovern, a molecular archaeologist at the University of Pennsylvania's Museum of Archaeology and Anthropology, found the excavated materials. McGovern is a world expert in ancient civilizations' drinks and foods; he analyzes these materials at a molecular level to determine what they consist of.

McGovern was able to determine the types of food and drink served at the funeral feast. The drink in the large vessels was a combination of a honey mead, wine, and beer. It was about 10 percent alcohol by volume. McGovern guessed that the bittering agent he found was saffron, based on the spices that were commonly used in the region at that time. The spice would have given the drink a golden look.

While McGovern was a world-renowned molecular archeologist, he was not a home brewer. That task fell to others. During a dinner for Michael Jackson, a famous writer on the subject of beer (not the late music figure), McGovern mentioned that he had been working on the elixir puzzle but did not know how to properly recreate it.

Connecticut home brewers and authors of *Clone Brews* and *Beer Captured*, Tess and Mark Szamatulski, stepped up to the task. They began to experiment with what they thought may have been the constituents in this historical elixir. First, they created a brew that contained Muscat grape juice along with wild thyme honey and barley malt. This original concoction was about 8% alcohol by volume.

After this original experiment, the owner of the Dogfish Head Craft Brewery in Delaware agreed to make a larger batch of this funeral drink. Sam Calagione, the proprietor of the Dogfish Head Craft Brewery, used the same blend of ingredients to create a 93-gallon batch in which he added Indian saffron for added flavor and color, and used mead yeast to ferment it.

This funeral feast drink, now dubbed Midas Touch Golden Elixir, was served at a $150-per-person benefit dinner for University of

Pennsylvania's Molecular Archaeology Program in 2001. It was 7% ABV, compared to the original 10% of the historic drink. It was such a success that Dogfish Head Brewery continued to brew small quantities to a test market that was sold through their distribution network. The feedback was positive, and now the Midas Touch Golden Elixir is a regular offering by the micro-brewery; the ABV is 9%. While the original test market batch was packaged in 750-ml. corked Champagne bottles, it is now sold in regular beer bottles and released in limited quantities monthly. This chapter includes the cloned recipe so you can make this special historic brew at home. While it contains elements of a mead and beer, the Muscat grapes provide the base of the drink and can therefore be thought of as a wine. It contains unusual ingredients, and it is not a recipe to try the first time you try to make a fermented beverage. It is quite delicious, and your friends and family will talk about it for years.

In 2003, a group of friends and I recreated our own version of King Midas' funeral feast as a Halloween party. We sat a plastic skeleton at the head of the table with fake gold coins strewn about him. All of the plates and utensils were gold-colored, as was the tablecloth and other decorations. The evening was complete with a belly dancer. Different people created each of the foods that were part of the original funeral feast. I created the golden elixir in honor of the occasion.

This brew is sparkling and therefore regular wine bottles and corks will not be able to handle the CO_2 pressure. You will need to store this in beer bottles, so you will need bottles, caps and a capper. These items are not much of an extra expense, and if you ever want to try your hand at creating beer, you will have to invest in a capper anyway.

The final elixir will have a golden color and will be slightly carbonated. It is great with Greek and Mediterranean dishes. Try serving it with a meal that includes Greek salad, gyros, and souvlaki.

Some of the ingredients, like the malt extracts, are actually used in beer making, so they can be easily found at the same suppliers for winemaking supplies, as they often supply home beer making ingredients as well. This is an unusual drink in that it is technically a wine, a beer, and a mead.

Touch of Gold Mead

Yield 5 gallons
OG = 1.078 FG = 1.010 ABV = 9%
Original Brix (19.00) - Final Brix (2.25) = 16.75 x 0.55 =
9% ABV

Ingredients:

3 ⅓ lbs. Briess light malt extract syrup
1 ½ lbs. Briess light dry malt extract
3 lbs. honey (do not boil)
2 lbs. Alexander's Muscat grape concentrate (do not boil)
½ tsp. dry saffron (boil 15 minutes)
½ oz. 2.5 AAU* Willamette hops (bittering hop) (5% alpha acid)
½ oz. 2.5 AAU Willamette hops (flavor hop) (5% alpha acid)
1 tsp. Irish moss
White Labs WLP500 (Trappist) or Wyeast 3787 (Trappist) yeast
(note that these are beer yeasts)

¾ cup of corn sugar (for priming)
Water (enough to make 5 gallons of wine must)
Standard winemaking equipment
55, 12-oz. beer bottles
Unused bottle caps
Bottle capper
Cheesecloth

*AAU (alpha acid units): This is a measure of bitterness of a hops. The higher the number, the more bitter the hops are.

Instructions:

1. Bring 2 ½ gallons of water to a rolling boil. Take the pot off the heat and add the malt syrup and powder. Stir it vigorously until it is dissolved. Do not return to the heat until it is dissolved, or it will scorch on the bottom of the pot. When syrup and powder are dissolved, return the pot to the heat and bring back to a boil.

2. Add flavor hops and Irish moss to pot and allow to boil for 60 minutes. When there is 15 minutes left of the boil, add bittering hops and the saffron.

3. Take pot off the heat and stir in the honey to completely dissolve.

4. Pour liquid through cheesecloth to strain out the hops. Pour the hot liquid into the fermenter with 2 gallons cold water. Add the grape concentrate to this mixture. Rinse the can with a little hot water to get all of the concentrate out.

5. Bring the liquid level to 5 ½ gallons with cool water. Allow mixture to cool to at least 80 degrees F before pitching the yeast.

6. Keep must between 68 to 70 degrees F and allow to ferment for ten to 14 days.

7. After fermentation has slowed, rack into secondary vessel and allow to sit for 24 hours.

8. Add corn sugar to mixture and stir until it is dissolved.

9. Bottle your wine in beer bottles and caps. This will be carbonated, so regular wine bottles and corks will explode.

10. Allow wine to age for a month before drinking.

All-Grain Recipe

If you are an experienced beer maker, you might try the using an all-grain recipe in which you would use 6 lbs. of two-row pale malt instead of 3 ⅓ lbs. Briess light malt extract syrup. Mashing is a process in which you use hot water to extract the sugars from the grains. This requires specific equipment such as a masher. In this recipe, you would mash your grains at 155 degrees F for 45 minutes. This is done by holding the temperature of the boiled water that has been added to the grain for the specified number of minutes. Use a brew belt or similar device, and put a specialized brew pot on the stovetop. You should use a thermometer to monitor your progress and to make changes as needed. You should also consider reducing the bittering hops at the end to 0.4 ounces.

Modern cultural references to mead:

In the book *American Gods*, by Neil Gaiman: The main character drinks mead, which he finds foul-tasting, to seal a deal. It is the favorite drink of the main character in Neil Gaiman's *Sandman* series as well.

The Wolves of Willoughby Chase, by Joan Aiken: The characters Bonnie and Sylvia are given metheglin to give them inspiration for their walk.

Eragon book series, by Christopher Paolini: Mead is the common drink in this book and those that followed in the series.

Harry Potter and the Half-Blood Prince, by J.K. Rowling: In the story, Professor Slughorn gives Harry and Ron some mead that was meant for a Christmas gift to Dumbledore; Ron almost dies because it had been poisoned.

Gravity's Rainbow, by Thomas Pynchon: One of the characters makes banana mead and serves it for breakfast.

Simple Mead

Yield 5 gallons 19/L

OG = 1.140 FG = 1.045 ABV = 10%

Original Brix (29.25) - Final Brix (11) = 18.25 x 0.55 = 10% ABV

Ingredients:

18 lbs. wildflower honey

2 cups New York maple syrup, Grade A

32 oz. fresh lemon and lime juice (you will use some pulp)

12 lemons

8 limes

4 pieces (⅛ fruit) orange peel

5 pieces tangerine peel

3 pieces lemon peel

2 oz. coriander

Water (enough to make 5 gallons of wine must)

Sweet mead yeast

Standard winemaking equipment

½ tsp. gypsum

½ tsp. calcium carbonate

¼ tsp. sea salt

Standard winemaking equipment

Instructions:

1. Boil about 4 gallons of water. Treat it with gypsum, calcium carbonate, and sea salt. Boil it for 30 min. Take off the heat and add orange peels, lime peels, and ½ ounce coriander. Allow the mixture to cool to 90 degrees C/194 degrees F. Add honey and maple syrup. Allow temperature to drop to 80 degrees C/176 degrees F. Add strained juice from six lemons and four limes.

2. Stir for 30 minutes. Raise temperature back up to 90 degrees C/194 degrees F. Add juice with pulp — six more lemons and four limes.

3. Reduce the temperature of mixture quickly either by ice bath or wort chiller. Reduce temperature quickly and place in primary fermenter. Allow to ferment for two weeks.

4. Rack to carboy. Allow to sit for two months, then bottle.

5. The longer you allow it to mature, the smoother the taste.

Toasts from around the world:

Irish (Gaelic): Sláinte! (to your health)

Hebrew: Le'chaim! (to life)

French: Santé! (health)

English: Cheers!

Spanish: Salud! (health)

Italian: Salute (health)

Chinese: Ganbei! (dry your cup)

Dutch: Prost! (health)

German: Prost! (cheers)

Welsh: Iechyd da! (health)

Russian: Vashe zdorovie! (to health)

Japanese: Kanpai! (dry your cup)

Raspberry Cyser

Yield 1 gallon/3.8 L

OG = 1.090 FG = 1.014 ABV = 10%

Original Brix (21.75) - Final Brix (3.50) = 18.25 x 0.55 = 10% ABV

Ingredients:

5 gallons frozen apple juice

24 lbs. of a local raw honey

2 lbs. fresh raspberries

Red Star Cuvee yeast

Water (enough to make 1 gallon of wine must)

Standard winemaking equipment

Instructions:

1. Freeze the raspberries, as this will make it easier to press the juice from them. Before you use them in the recipe, make sure they are thawed. Place honey in a pot with 3 quarts of water and boil for 20 minutes. Skim foam off the top. Add apple juice and boil for another ten minutes.

2. Place raspberries in cheesecloth in the fermenter and pour the honey/apple mixture over the top. Try to cool the mixture quickly. Add pectic enzyme.

3. When the must reaches room temperature, pitch the yeast. Allow it to ferment for three weeks.

4. Rack the mead off the bag and squeeze juice gently from the cheesecloth.

5. For dry mead, allow the mead to sit in a dark, cool place for four to six months. Rack every three weeks until mead is clear. Bottle when wine is ready.

Cyser

A cyser is a type of mead that contains apple juice as a primary ingredient.

Yield 1 gallon/ 3.8 L
OG = 1.090 FG = 1.014 ABV = 10%
Original Brix (21.75) - Final Brix (3.50) = 18.25 x 0.55 = 10% ABV

Ingredients:

2 ½ lbs. orange blossom honey
½ gallon unsweetened 100% apple juice
Water (enough to make 1 gallon of wine must)
Champagne yeast
Standard winemaking equipment
1-gallon carboy

Instructions:

1. Boil the honey in 3 quarts of water. Skim off foam as it forms. Remove from heat and add juice and nutrient. Allow to cool for 24 hours.

2. Pitch the yeast and transfer to carboy.

3. Allow to ferment for three weeks and rack off the sediment.

4. If you wish to add carbonation, you can add ¼ teaspoon of white table sugar per 12-ounce bottle, or stir in ½ lb. to 1 lb. raw of honey. You will want to dissolve the honey in boiling water first and cool it. Rack every three weeks until mead is clear.

5. Once you are sure that the mead is stable, add a Campden table. Allow to sit for another week. Take hydrometer readings to make sure that the mead has not refermented. Bottle.

6. Allow this mead to mature three to six months before drinking.

Pyment

Yield: 5 gallons/19 L
OG = 1.100 FG = 1.010 ABV = 10%
Original Brix (24.00) - Final Brix (5.75) = 18.25 x 0.55 = 10% ABV

Ingredients:

13 ½ lbs. clover honey
12 lbs. local wine grapes (crush by hand)
2 tsp. yeast nutrient
Water
Mead yeast
Standard winemaking equipment
Nylon bag or cheesecloth

Instructions:

1. Boil the honey in 3 quarts of water. Skim off foam as it forms. Remove from heat and add grapes into bag/cloth. Squeeze gently by hand into fermenter and place bag in the fermenter. Add remaining ingredients except the yeast. Allow to cool for 24 hours.

2. Pitch the yeast and transfer to carboy.

3. Allow to ferment for three weeks and rack off the sediment and remove grape bag.

4. For dry mead, allow the mead to sit in a dark, cool place for four to six months. Rack every three weeks until mead is clear. Bottle when wine is ready.

5. If you wish to add carbonation, you can add ¼ teaspoon of white table sugar per 12-ounce bottle, or stir in ½ lb. to 1 lb. of raw honey. Dissolve the honey in boiling water first and cool it. Rack every three weeks until mead is clear.

6. Allow mead to age for six months to a year.

A Hippocras is a type of spiced wine. The following is a recipe using the pyment; however, you can use most any red wine in the recipe.

For every gallon of wine:

1 ⅛ tsp. ground cinnamon
¼ tsp. ground ginger
⅜ tsp. ground cloves
¾ tsp. ground nutmeg
¾ tsp. marjoram
¾ tsp. cracked cardamom
¾ tsp. black pepper

Stir ingredients into the wine. You can even serve the wine hot.

Concord Grape Pyment

Yield: 5 gallons/19 L
OG = 1.100 FG = 1.010 ABV = 10% ABV
Original Brix (24.00) - Final Brix (5.75) = 18.25 x 0.55 = 10% ABV

Ingredients:

15 lbs. honey (clover, orange blossom, or any other light-flavored honey)
120 oz. Concord grape concentrate

5 tsp. yeast nutrient
1 ¼ tsp. yeast energizer
1 Campden tablet
Sweet mead yeast
Standard winemaking equipment
Water (enough to make 5 gallons of wine must)

Instructions:

1. Boil the honey in 3 quarts of water. Skim off foam as it forms. Remove from heat and add all of the ingredients except the yeast and grape juice. Allow to cool for 24 hours.

2. Pitch the yeast and transfer to carboy.

3. Allow to ferment for three weeks and rack off the sediment.

4. Boil juice for ten minutes. Add a Campden tablet and the juice to the mead.

5. For dry mead, allow the mead to sit in a dark, cool place four to six months. Rack every three weeks until mead is clear. Bottle when wine is ready.

6. If you wish to add carbonation, you can add ¼ teaspoon of white table sugar per 12-ounce bottle, or stir in ½ lb. to 1 lb. raw of honey. You will want to dissolve the honey in boiling water first and cool it. Rack every three weeks until mead is clear.

7. Allow mead to age for six months to a year.

Peach Pyment

Yield 1 gallon/ 3.8 L

OG = 1.090 FG = 1.014 ABV = 10%

Original Brix (22.00) - Final Brix (3.75) = 18.25 x 0.55 = 10% ABV

Ingredients:

2-qt. bottle of Welch's White Grape/Peach juice

2 lbs. honey

Red Star "Cote de Baum" yeast

1 tsp. yeast nutrient

1 ¼ tsp. yeast energizer

1 Campden tablet

Standard winemaking equipment

Water (enough to make 1 gallon of wine must)

Instructions:

1. Boil the honey in 3 quarts of water. Skim off foam as it forms. Remove from heat and add all of the ingredients except the yeast and grape juice. Allow to cool for 24 hours.

2. Pitch the yeast and transfer to carboy.

3. Allow to ferment for three weeks and rack off the sediment.

4. Boil juice for ten minutes. Add a Campden tablet and the juice to the mead.

5. For dry mead, allow the mead to sit in a dark, cool place for four to six months. Rack every three weeks until mead is clear. Bottle when wine is ready.

6. If you wish to add carbonation, you can add ¼ teaspoon of white table sugar per 12-ounce bottle, or stir in ½ lb. to 1 lb. raw of honey. You will want to dissolve the honey in boiling water first and cool it. Rack every three weeks until mead is clear.

7. Allow mead to age for six months to a year.

Orange Melomel

Yield 1 gallon/3.8 L
OG = 1.090 FG = 1.014 ABV = 10%
Original Brix (22.00) - Final Brix (3.75) = 18.25 x 0.55 = 10% ABV

Ingredients:

4 lbs. raw orange blossom honey
Water
1 packet Champagne yeast
Citrus peels
2 cups freshly squeezed orange or tangerine juice
Standard winemaking equipment

Instructions:

1. Boil the honey in 3 quarts of water. Skim off foam as it forms. Remove from heat and add all of the ingredients except the yeast and orange juice. Allow to cool for 24 hours.

2. Pitch the yeast and transfer to carboy.

3. Allow to ferment for three weeks and rack off
    the sediment.

4. Boil juice for ten minutes. Add a Campden tablet and the
    juice to the mead.

5. For dry mead, allow the mead to sit in a dark, cool place
    for four to six months. Rack every three weeks until
    mead is clear. Bottle when wine is ready.

6. If you wish to add carbonation, you can add ¼ teaspoon
    of white table sugar per 12-ounce bottle, or stir in ½ lb.
    to 1 lb. of raw honey. You will want to dissolve the honey
    in boiling water first and cool it. Rack every three weeks
    until mead is clear.

7. Allow mead to age for six months to a year.

Sack Mead

Yield 1 gallon/ 3.8 L
OG = 1.090 FG = 1.014 ABV = 10%
Original Brix (22.00) - Final Brix (3.75) = 18.25 x 0.55 = 10% ABV

Ingredients:

3 lbs. orange blossom honey
1 tsp. acid blend
1 tsp. pectic enzyme
1 Campden tablet
1 package Montrachet yeast
1 tsp. yeast nutrient

1 ½ cups orange juice at room temperature
¼ tsp. grape tannin
Standard winemaking equipment

Instructions:

1. Boil the honey in 3 quarts of water. Skim off foam as it forms. Remove from heat and add all of the ingredients except the yeast and orange juice. Allow to cool for 24 hours.

2. Pitch the yeast and transfer to carboy.

3. Allow to ferment for three weeks and rack off the sediment.

4. Boil juice for ten minutes. Add a Campden tablet and the juice to the mead.

5. For dry mead allow the mead to sit in a dark, cool place for four to six months. Rack every three weeks until mead is clear. Bottle when wine is ready.

6. If you wish to add carbonation, you can add ¼ teaspoon of white table sugar per 12-ounce bottle, or stir in ½ lb. to 1 lb. raw of honey. Dissolve the honey in boiling water first and cool it. Rack every three weeks until mead is clear.

7. Allow mead to age for six months to a year.

Pomegranate Melomel

Yield: 5 gallons/19 L

OG = 1.100 FG = 1.010 ABV = 10%

Original Brix (24.00) - Final Brix (5.75) = 18.25 x 0.55 = 10% ABV

Ingredients:

10 lbs. orange blossom honey

5 lbs. wildflower honey

2 tsp. yeast nutrient

Champagne yeast

Water (enough to make 5 gallons of wine must)

Standard winemaking equipment

1 gallon of pomegranate juice (can be pure juice from the store or made from 14 lbs. of pomegranates)

Instructions:

1. Boil the honey in 3 quarts of water. Skim off foam as it forms. Remove from heat and add all of the ingredients except the yeast and pomegranate juice. Allow to cool for 24 hours.

2. Pitch the yeast and transfer to carboy.

3. Allow to ferment for three weeks and rack off the sediment.

4. Boil pomegranate juice for ten minutes. If you are using fresh pomegranates, you must squeeze the juice and discard the seeds and pitch. This can be a little labor-intensive. Add a Campden tablet and juice to the mead.

5. For dry mead, allow the mead to sit in a dark, cool place for four to six months. Rack every three weeks until mead is clear. Bottle when wine is ready.

6. If you wish to add carbonation, you can add ¼ teaspoon of white table sugar per 12-ounce bottle, or stir in ½ lb. to 1 lb. raw of honey. You will want to dissolve the honey in boiling water first and cool it. Rack every three weeks until mead is clear.

7. Allow mead to age for six months to a year.

Orange Ginger Mead

Yield: 5 gallons/19 L
OG = 1.100 FG = 1.010 ABV = 10%
Original Brix (24.00) - Final Brix (5.75) = 18.25 x 0.55 = 10% ABV

Ingredients:

11 ½ lbs. wildflower honey
6 oz. macerated ginger
12-oz. can frozen orange juice
Water (enough to produce 5 gallons of wine)
Lalvin EC-1118 yeast
Standard winemaking equipment

Instructions:

1. Boil the honey in 3 quarts of water. Skim off foam as it forms. Boil for 30 minutes. Add 6 ounces ginger and the orange juice. Let it sit for another 30 minutes on the stove with no heat. Add to fermenter and bring up the level to 5 gallons. Allow to cool for 24 hours.

2. Pitch the yeast and transfer to carboy.

3. Allow to ferment for three weeks and rack off the sediment.

4. For dry mead, allow the mead to sit in a dark, cool place for four to six months. Rack every three weeks until mead is clear. Bottle when the mead is ready.

5. If you wish to add carbonation, you can add ¼ teaspoon of white table sugar per 12-ounce bottle, or stir in ½ lb. to 1 lb. raw of honey. Dissolve the honey in boiling water first and cool it. Rack every three weeks until mead is clear.

6. Allow mead to age for six months to a year.

CHAPTER 9

Adding a Creative Touch

> "Whenever a man is tired, wine is a great restorer of strength."
> — Homer, *The Iliad*

CHOOSING A NAME

Creating a name for your wine can be almost as fun as creating the wine. You can name it anything you want — it is your wine. The name should fit the character of the wine, unless you are trying to be humorous. For instance you would not want to name a delicate dessert wine "Big Red, In-Your-Face Bullfighter's Wine."

You can be simple and just add your name, such as "John's Oaked Chardonnay" or "Peragine Estates 2009 Merlot."

Wine is a great gift at the holidays or special events. You can name your wine according to the season:

Santa's Big Red Hat

Elf Grog
Rudolf Fell off the Roof Viognier
The Great Pumpkin Mead
Thanks for Giving me Wine
Anniversary Celebration Chambourcin

You can name your wine after famous people:

Obama's Election Ballot
Palin's Punch
Einstein's Theory
Franklin's Electric Jolt

Literature and movies provide a great resource of wine names:

Indiana Jones Next Adventure
Star Wars Cantina House Wine
Homer's Next Epic
Jane Austen's Romance in a Bottle
Mary Shelley's Frankenwine

Many people name their wines after their favorite pets, their children, and even their best friends. However, if you choose a potentially offensive title, even if you think it is humorous, it could be difficult to share or give as a gift. Take time and taste your wine before naming it. Giving a wine a name is giving it an identity.

FANCY LABELS

Once you have decided on a name, think about putting it on a label. Labels can get very creative because you can make whatever style or design you would like, and wine competitions even have label contests. You can buy pre-gummed labels to decorate, wet, and stick on. Plain sheets of this label paper are available to buy and use in your own printer — you get to have fun decorating them. One of the advantages to this paper is that it will not disintegrate when it comes into contact with liquid. Some of the premade labels and label paper can be a little pricey, and some people — myself included — use regular printer paper and school paste to put on the labels. This is for two reasons: After making thousands of bottles, I got a little tired of making fancy labels, and paste comes off a bottle a lot easier than a pre-gummed label. Labels can really dress up a bottle and make better gifts when they are nicely packaged.

There are a number of wine label programs available on the Internet for download. These allow you to customize your labels and make them look professional:

The Vintner's Marketplace: **www.vinetowine.com**
Best Vista Downloads: **www.bestvistadownloads.com**
Soft Platz: **www.softplatz.com/Soft/Business/Other/ Visual-Labels.html**
Stoney Creek Wine Press: **www.stoneycreekwinepress.com**
Super Shareware: **www.supershareware.com/info/gliftic.html**
Software Directory 3D2F: **http://3d2f.com/programs/7-915-wine-organizer-download.shtml**

If you do not want to do it all yourself, you can order custom-made labels. With custom labels, you can add photos and any other personal images to your wine label. These services make attractive labels, but they can be a little pricey:

Classic Studio Labels: **www.classicstudiolabels.com** ($1.50 per label)

My Own Labels: **www.myownlabels.com** ($1 per label)

One of the things you will want to decide is whether you want just one front label, a front and back label, or if you wish to include a bottleneck label.

SHRINK CAPSULES

These are the fancy covers that go over a cork on top of the bottle. They come in a variety of colors and are easy to attach to your bottle. They will sit loose on top of your bottle until you aim a hot hair dryer on them; then they will shrink into place. They add a nice, professional touch to your wine. They peel off easily when you are ready to drink your wine and cost about $5 for 30 of them. You can also invest in a cap shrinker, but these are expensive and do not do a better job than a hair dryer.

Champagne foils

If you decide to make Champagne and you have put in the special cork and secured it with a wire, you may want to cover the top with a foil. These are easy to apply and they come in a number of different colors.

Bottle-sealing wax

You can top your bottle off with colored wax that provides a moisture-resistant barrier that will keep your wine fresh and help prevent spoilage. The wax comes in many different colors and is packaged as small beads.

In order to use the wax, you will need a double boiler. Place the wax beads in the top pan over boiling water. Keep the wax moving by stirring. When it is liquid, dip the corked wine into the wax. You may want to let it cool for a few seconds and add a second coat or more to the bottle. These waxes can really brighten the appearance of your bottle.

If you have a signet ring, you can press into the wax on top to add another creative touch to your wine. Make sure you do it before the wax hardens.

WINE JOURNAL

Creating a winemaking journal is one way to keep up with your winemaking recipes and to record your successes and failures. There are ones you can buy at a bookstore, but it is just as easy to copy the next page and make one of your own. You can even create a virtual version to keep on your computer. You can paste a copy of the label on the page.

Name of wine: _____
Rating of this wine (scale 1-10, 1 being worst ever, 10 being best): ___
Date it was begun: _____
OG or starting Brix: _____
Yeast type: _____
FG or final Brix: _____

Ingredients:

Instructions:

Hydrometer readings:
Date: Reading:

Temperature readings:
Date: Reading:

Acid readings:
Date: Reading:

Hydrogen sulfite readings:
Date: Reading:

pH readings:
Date: Reading:

Notes:

Problems:
How I fixed it:

Changes in future batches:

Reviews of wine:

Date was first tasted:
Where it was first tasted:

This is just a template, and you can be as creative as you want. However, you may want to take some steps to waterproof your journal. Wrap it in food wrap or place it in a zippable plastic bag when you refer to it on winemaking days. You can also use a cookbook stand. If you are using a virtual version on your laptop, you can buy screen protectors and keyboard protectors. You can also place your laptop in an extra large zippable plastic bag and put a rubber elastic band around it to make it snug.

You can add some photos of your winemaking process and even some of you and your friends drinking the wine. A journal can be a fun thing to create, but it can also contain all of your important winemaking recipes and secrets.

WINE BOX

One of the problems I faced once I created wine and bottled it was that I had no place to put the bottles. I went to a local craft store and bought a number of wooden craft crates. They are durable and can hold a case of wine. The best part is that they have handles. These boxes are unfinished wood, so if you want to paint or decorate them, you can. I let my children paint and decorate a couple of them. This allowed them to be a part of the winemaking process, and whenever I look at the crates, I smile.

They stack easily when full of wine. You can also add casters and wheels on the bottom for easier mobility, and add a handle or a rope to the front to pull it.

CHAPTER 10

Creating a Home Vineyard

"Clearly, the pleasures wines afford are transitory — but so are those of the ballet, or of a musical performance. Wine is inspiring and adds greatly to the joy of living."

— Napoleon Bonaparte, French political leader

"There is a long process to pick just the right location for the vineyard. The right combination of location and the winemaker will produce a world-class wine. It has been the right combination of cold-climate grapes, choosing the right clones, and nurturing the vines that are the basis of producing great fruit."

— Eileen Crane, winemaker and president;
Domaine Carneros Vineyards

One of the first things to consider in creating a home vineyard is what kinds of grapes will grow where you want to place your vines. As you will learn, there are certain soil conditions and sun exposures to consider when planting your vines. Currently, there are more than 3,000 commercial vineyards functioning in the United States. Each state has at least one winery, so it is possible to grow vines almost anywhere in the United States. Most of the wine production in the United States occurs in three states: Oregon, Washington, and California. If you live in theses states, you benefit from a conducive climate and viticultural tradition. The chart below lists some of the other regions in United States where grapes are cultivated. These are worth mentioning because these states are among the best for cultivating a home vineyard.

Area of the United States	States that are the best for starting a home vineyard
Southwest	Texas and New Mexico
Midwest	Missouri, Illinois, and Minnesota
Rocky Mountain region	Idaho and Colorado
Great Lakes region	Michigan, Northern New York, and Ohio
East Coast	New Jersey, New York State, Pennsylvania, Virginia, and North Carolina

APPELLATION REGIONS

There are particular areas in the previously mentioned states that are considered appellation, or "Viticultural," regions. Appellation designations are used to establish the agricultural boundaries of different growing regions in states and counties according to where vineyards are planted. The system in the United States has similarities to those in countries such as France, where certain wines can only be labeled as an appellation wine. An example is Champagne, which can only be labeled as Champagne if the grapes are grown in that area of France. Wineries such as the Biltmore Estates can produce what they label as sparkling wines, but only wines created in the Champagne appellation in France can be called Champagne.

The history of wine appellations reaches back to the Bible, where it uses references to the wine of Samaria, wine of Carmel, wine of Jezreel, and the wine of Helbon. Appellations continued through the Middle Ages; although there were no strict rules, it was more of a system to describe where a particular wine came from. In 1730, in Tokaj-Hegyalja, Hungary, the first official sanctioned appellation rules were created.

In the United States, it was not until 1978 that the Bureau of Alcohol, Tobacco and Firearms, now known as the Alcohol and Tobacco Tax and Trade Bureau, established American Viticultural Areas (AVA). These areas exist on different climates and geographical features. In 1980, when the Augusta AVA in Missouri was created, the Bureau of Alcohol Tobacco and Firearms created new regulations were. Today, there are more than 187 different official AVAs in the United States.

In order for a wine to be labeled to have come from a certain AVA region, the wine must be include at least 85 percent of the grapes from that particular region. There are also local county rules that can be applied, such as that some counties only require that 75 percent come from that county for labeling purposes. Some bottles may have multicounty designations, with each county percentage on the label. Some states also have their own requirements — for example, wines from Texas must contain at least 85 percent of grapes from that state, whereas California requires 100 percent.

The appellation of American or U.S. wine is not used very often to describe wine sold in the United States. It is a designation that is usually used for wines that are exported to other countries — even then, it cannot include a vintage year. If you are going to start your own winery, choose the types of grapes you want to grow or buy. If you intend to use a certain appellation, such as "North Carolina Wine," then you cannot buy the bulk of your grapes from Georgia.

There are some special wines in America, such as "American Burgundy" or "California Champagne." These names cannot be used in Europe due to strict appellation rules that state only wines from particular reasons can have the names of Burgundy and Champagne. These types of names must have an origin name, such as California, to go along with the generic terms, such as Burgundy.

Other generic names that can be paired with regions in the United States include Claret, Chablis, Chianti, Madeira, Malaga, Marsala, Moselle, Port, Rhine wine, Sauternes, Sauterne or Haut Sauterne, Sherry, and Tokay.

Once you determine what your particular appellation region is, the next thing to consider is what kinds of grapes will grow the best. You could look at what grapes are doing well in your region by visiting other local wineries and vineyards. Ask the owners about their success and failures with certain varieties of vines. You may even be able to broker a deal in which you will be able to buy some of their harvested grapes while you are waiting for your vines to mature enough to harvest.

"The ground in the Yadkin Valley Appellation is great to grow grape vines because of its red clay composition and the slight tobacco-earthy tone it imparts to the wine."

— Drew Renegar, general manager;
Allison Oaks Vineyards

BUILDING A TRELLIS SYSTEM

"After a hail storm destroyed a good part of our crop, I learned nets are necessary to protect the vines."

— John Langley, owner; Urraca Wines

The good news about building a trellis system at home is that all of the supplies can be bought at your local hardware store. Grape vines must be trained upward on wires that are attached to poles in the ground. This prevents the vines from growing out of control or touching the ground, which will risk the fruit rotting. It is hard work, but most people with basic building skills it can do this. The following is a list of materials you might need with building a trellis. The actual materials will depend on the type of trellis you intend to build.

Trellis supplies:

Springs

Ratchets

Earth anchors

Cross arms

Wire fasteners

Wire splicers

Fence pliers

Spinning jenny

Posthole digger

Tamper

Shovel

Saw

Step 1:

The first thing you must decide is where in your yard the trellis will go. If you have a lot of land and can choose a spot that has good drainage and is protected from frost, then this would be ideal. You can choose a fancy arbor design, or something that is more functional. This depends on your budget and skills at building.

Consider whether the grapes will get enough light. They need this in order to flower and produce grapes. Grapes grown in the shade will not do well; look for a place they will get full sunlight. This is also important for the development of new buds on growing canes for grapes to be able to flourish year to year. A cane is the part of vine where the grapes grow. Light will also enable you to see the vines and grapes clearly to make sure they are growing properly and to know where you will need to prune. Full sunlight is defined as six to eight hours of direct sunlight.

It is important to have the trellis in an area that will discourage disease and fungal growth. Disease is one of the things that winemakers have to battle with when growing vines. Most European vines are not disease-resistant to American pests like Pierce's disease, a virus, and phylloxera, a root louse. This is why many of the vines are grafted on America rootstock: to make them stronger and more disease-resistant. Native varieties, such as Muscadine, are much more disease-resistant to the local pests. Contact a viticulturist or agricultural school such as University of California at Davis to determine which combination of root stock and clone of the varietal you want does well in your soil conditions.

Try to find an area that has good airflow and does not stay damp. Your trellis needs to keep the fruit off the ground in order to avoid soil-borne diseases that can rot the fruit.

You do not need a huge area to grow vines, but you will need enough space to get around the trellis and tend the grapes. You must decide on the system of trellising you will need, because there is more than one type, depending on the varietal you are growing.

There are three main types of vines that most home winemakers would grow: American, French-American grafts or occasional hybrids, and European, or *V. vinifera*. Each type of vine has its own way of growing.

American and hybrids tend to grow downward or have procumbent growth. This type of vine needs a trellis system that has a top wire, about 5 to 6 feet off the ground. This allows the vine to grow downward without touching the ground.

V. vinifera, including those that have been grafted to American rootstock vines, grow upward and do better with a vertical wiring system with a set of catch wires. If you have limited space, planting hybrids is your best bet. They are easier to tend, and the trellising system is much easier. It is this type of system that I will describe below.

Step 2:

Once you have decided where you will plant, decide how large the trellis will be. Space your posts about 10 to 12 feet apart. For instance, if you had about a 50-foot area to work with, you would need at least six posts.

Step 3:

Dig deeply with your post-hole digger. You may need someone with a backhoe to help if the ground is too hard. The holes need to be deep enough to support your base posts. The base posts should be 4 x 4-inch or 6 x 6-inch lumber or, preferably, a steel post because these are rot-proof and stronger. The length of the poles should be about 9 feet. Your hole should be at least 3 feet deep to steady the post upright.

Once you have the pole in the ground, you need to pack the dirt around it tightly. You can do this by using a tool to push dirt in the hole around the post and pack it in firmly. A hoe does the job nicely. Remember that you are going to space the poles about 10 to 12 feet apart.

Step 4:

Once the posts are firmly in the ground, attach the wire. The wire should be high-tensile, 12-gauge steel. A lighter gauge can break with the weight of the crop. Attach the wire to the top of the posts using heavy-duty staples or nails that you will need to bend over. Stretch the wire tightly between the posts.

Step 5:

Place the grafted root stock (seedlings) at the appropriate depth based on the graft union. If it is planted too high, the root stock will outgrow the grafted varietal and leave you with the wrong kind of grapes. They should be centered between the posts, not next to the posts. The center of the vine will grow strong and sturdily over the years, so there is no need to place it next to the post.

Next, tie a string from the top wire down to the vine. This will allow the tendrils of the new vine to train upward. They will continue to grow upward until they reach the horizontal cable on the top. As the vine grows, help the tendrils find the strings.

Step 6:

Pruning is important. There are several types of pruning, depending on the type of vine and trellis system. For this simple type of arbor, you will prune to one single parent vine. Pinch off anything that grows from this central vine. This will help the central vine to grow sturdy and strong. When it reaches the top where the cable is, it will naturally branch off.

You will need to train this growth of the central vine for the first three years. If you see grapes grow, just pinch them off. All of the plants' energy needs to be focused on that central Cordone structure for establishing a healthy root system.

Step 7:

When watering your vines, spray water on the base of the plant directly, and try not to get the foliage wet because this can promote mildew growth. A soaker hose works well for this task.

Your grape vine must have enough water to grow and produce healthy grapes.

As your new vines are growing, you need to water them more frequently, especially when new grape clusters begin to form. If you do not water the vine, the baby grapes will die off before they can mature.

Step 8:

For a small home vineyard, you can use a fertilizer that is 10-10-10 (10 percent nitrogen, 10 percent potash, 10 percent phosphate), or any fertilizer whose ratios are equal — such as an organic source, which might be 5-5-5 — from your local hardware or plant supply store. After the initial couple of years of vine growth, it should not be necessary to fertilize your vines as long as the soil is rich in humus. You can add some compost if you would like. As leaves die and drop to the ground, they will release nutrients back into the soil, so allow the leaves to decay without raking them up. Pull out the weeds, especially during the first couple of years of growth, so they are not competing with your vines.

Step 9:

In order to ensure that your grapes are not harmed, you may want to spray them with antifungal and insecticides. As your grapes mature, you will also want to protect them from animals and birds. Buy netting and cover the vines once grapes begin to appear and ripen.

That is a basic trellising system. If you plan to grow a larger crop, it is best to find a professional or another winemaker to help you out.

"We planted our vines and waited about three years for them to mature. The first wines we created were still young wines because the vines need to mature even more. The older the vines are, the more mature their fruit, so we anticipate even better vintages in the future."

— Drew Renegar, general manager; Allison Oaks Vineyards

PRUNING

Pruning grapes is essential for their growth and maturity. Without pruning, the previous year's growth will compete with the plants' energy, and new grapes will not grow to maturity. Sometimes as much as 95 percent of the previous year's growth is removed. The new buds will produce too many grapes, which can overwork your vines. The more bunches of grapes that are on a vine, the more energy will be required to bring them to maturity. If this number is too high, the grapes will not mature at all.

The cutting back, or pruning of vines, actually stimulates proper growth. During the first few years of a new vine's growth, pruning is essential, as it is building strength and stability that will be important during fruit-producing years.

The good news is that the first year a vine is in the ground, you can take a break. Allow it to grow and pinch off shoots that are not part of the central vine This creates a central leader that will become your trunk — other than that, let it grow. This also allows the root system to grow and become established. It is, however, important to remove all the stems located near the base of the vine during the winter of the first year of growth. This is called "suckering," in which you remove the shoots growing from the latent buds of the root stock. Prune them as close to the main stem as possible. Allow the strongest stem that arises from above the graft union to remain. This will be the trunk of your vine from which you will create the cordons that hold the fruiting spurs. You should stake this over the winter.

The following spring, you will then "top" the central leader to the desired height at which you want the cordons to form.

As new shoots grow in the following spring, they should grow from the top of this new trunk. The shoots that come from the two top most buds will be trained onto the wires by pulling them horizontally and tying them to the wire. This is called "cordoning." Do not allow any other stalks to grow except these two. Choose two of the strongest stalks and prune off the rest. This is the beginning of the cordon. You will see new branches begin to grow off the main trunk, but you will need to prune ("sucker") these. You just want those two strong ones you left at the beginning of spring.

During the winter of the second year, you will see the basic shape of the vine: one upright trunk with two sets of side branches. During the third spring, you will just need to prune to this shape. All other branches should be pruned.

Once you reach the winter of the third year, and every other winter thereafter, leave about ten to 15 buds on each Cordon. These are the buds that will produce grapes the next year. These are referred to as renewal buds. Make sure each renewal bud has one to two leaf joints.

During the summer, your vines will grow. When the grape clusters begin to mature, prune some of the leaves to allow the grapes exposure to sunlight. Without the proper light and water, grapes will not be able to mature. During the late summer and early fall, it will be time to harvest the grapes. Use your palate and the tools, such as a pH testing kit and a hydrometer or refractometer, to calculate the sugar and acid content of your grapes to decide when the best time to pick is. Make sure you have all your winemaking equipment ready to go; you do not want the grapes to sit around for days after they have been harvested, as they could rot or develop diseases, not to mention attract thousands of fruit flies.

Chemicals and sprays for your vines:

"We do have to spray our vines with chemicals. We have found that only native American varietals can be organic because the European varietals are not accustomed to the diseases and insects in the United States; therefore, they need anti-fungal and pesticides to be sprayed on them."

— Drew Renegar, general manager;
Allison Oaks Vineyards

• • • • • • • • • • •

"There are organic methods that can be followed that do not require the use of fungicides and insecticides, but require a more proactive approach to vineyard management. Contact your local organic-farming vendors as a resource for organic farming techniques. You can also try to use IPM (integrated pest management) techniques, which work from the least toxic to most toxic methods to control the pest or disease infestation as needed."

— Suzanne Schellenberg, Hewitt Vineyard

• • • • • • • • • • •

"We use drip irrigation to grow our crops and traditional gutters to allow the water to reach the vines evenly and naturally."

— John Langley, owner; Urraca Wines

CHAPTER 11

The Next Step:
Open Your Own Winery

"Drink no longer water, but use a little wine for thy stomach's sake and thine often infirmities."

— 1 Timothy, 5:23

There is a saying in the wine business: "If you want to make a small fortune in the wine business, you have to start with a large one." It is a very expensive proposition and should not be entered into lightly.

If you are ready to start your own winery, keep in mind that it is a big step. Most of the winemakers I spoke with state it takes years and a lot of capital to get a winery on its feet. The steps that I present in this chapter are based upon North Carolina laws. You should check with your state before beginning your quest, so you do not miss anything or break any laws.

Advice for opening your winery and vineyard:

"Our best advice to someone who wants to open their own winery is to take baby steps. We understood there would be no profit in just growing the vines, but the process was long, and each piece we completed was another baby step forward. As we grow our winery business, we will continue to take small baby steps along the way."

— Drew Renegar, general manager; Allison Oaks Winery

• • • • • • • • • • •

"It takes quite a nest egg to start your own winery. Don't quit your day job right away. It could be ten years before a winery can make a noticeable profit."

— Mark Terry, general manager and winemaker; Westbend Winery

• • • • • • • • • • •

"You can invest a great fortune into just a little winery."

— John Langley, owner; Urraca Wines

STEPS TO FIRST CONSIDER

1. Make sure the property intended for your winery is properly zoned for that type of business. Check all city, county, and state laws concerning zoning.

2. Remember, under federal law you can make up to 200 gallons of wine per year per household, or 100 gallons for an individual, tax-exempt. If you produce more than this and intend to sell, you will have to pay taxes.

3. Before you open your doors as a winery, you must have your winery inspected by the federal Alcohol and

Tobacco Tax and Trade Bureau (TTB, formerly BATF).
They determine if you can obtain your final permit. It can
take about six months to a year get your TTB and your
ABC permits.

The following are steps to obtaining your winery permit:

1. Visit the TTB's "Forms" section of their Web site at
    www.ttb.gov/tax_audit/permits.shtml. Search for the
    following forms:

    a. Bonded winery license

    b. Facility inspection

    c. Label approval for each label (each type wine, each
        year) (Note that in some states, like North Carolina, it
        is not necessary for the TTB to approve a label if the
        wines are going to be exclusively sold in that state.
        However, it is still a good idea to get approval)

2. The section titled "Applications and Information Packets
    for Operating in the TTB Regulated Industries" will point
    you to a link for "Winery/Taxpaid Wine Bottling House"

3. Corporations, limited liability companies, and limited
    partnerships must register with their state's secretary
    of state. You should determine what type of ownership
    you wish to have and obtain appropriate Articles of
    Corporation, operating agreement, and so on

4. You will need a number of licenses in order to sell, distribute, and even have people taste wine. What you need to apply for:

   a. City wine license from your local city hall, if your winery exists in city limits

   b. County wine license, which you can obtain from your county courthouse tax collector division

   c. State wine tax license from your department of revenue

   d. Contact whatever similar agency you have to an Alcoholic Beverage Control Commission (ABC) to obtain:

      i. Resident unfortified winery permit ("on" or "off" premises). (For wineries, it is not usually necessary to have a resident limited winery permit. This is because people are just sampling your wines)

      ii. If you are selling wine by the glass or are having events in which you charge people to attend, then you will need a winery special-event permit

      iii. Label approval applications and distribution agreement forms

5. You will need to submit the following information and forms to ABC:

a. Applications and supporting materials for all applicable permits

b. A wine analysis containing the type of wine and the vintage additions and deletions for each label

c. A label approval form containing the wine type and vintage for each label

d. If you have people physically selling or soliciting orders, you will need a vendor representative permit for each

6. You should have one set of hard copies of these or similar forms:

   1. Alcoholic Beverage Control Laws of N.C. *(or your state)*

   2. N.C. Alcoholic Beverage Control Commission Rules *(or your state)*

   3. Code of Federal Regulations, 27 CFR Parts 1, 6, 8, 11, 9, and 240

7. Develop a wastewater management plan for your winery and check with state and federal laws concerning environmental legislation to make sure you are in compliance

8. Check with your state concerning any legal issues and shipping issues within and outside your state

As you can see, there is much more than just making wine and selling it. There are many legal hurdles you must overcome in order to open your doors. If you skip, ignore, or do any of the steps incorrectly, not only will your winery be shut down, but also you could potentially face fines and even incarceration.

The Alcohol and Tobacco TTB:

"Some people think it is really hard to go through all the hoops with the Alcohol and Tobacco Tax and Trade Bureau to get your license to sell or serve alcohol. My father read all the materials online and was able to do it by himself. There were other wineries that had hired an attorney on retainer for months without any movement. My father has helped them through the process as well. It is important to read and understand the material. They can be a little picky about labels, and sometimes we had to submit labels a couple of times before they were approved."

— Drew Renegar, general manager;
Allison Oaks Vineyards

RESEARCH BEFORE OPENING YOUR WINERY

There are several factors every proprietor needs to consider before opening and operating his or her business, aside from the forms you need specifically for a winery. Web sites and books on opening and operating a business are included in the resources section of this book. Consider each of the following:

- **Market area research:** What are good areas in your state to grow grapes and start a winery? Is there competition in your area?

- **Demographics:** Will the people in your area respond positively to a winery? What is the typical income and standard of living in your area? You will need to consider these when pricing your product.

- **Determine the legal structure of your business:** Proprietorship, general partnership, limited liability company, corporation, and S corporation are all common forms of businesses.

- **Prepare a business plan:** Executive summary, market analysis, company description, organization and management, marketing, sales management, services, products, financials, labor, startup costs, and funding requests should all go in the business plan.

- **Your office:** Will you have an office to operate your accounting, organization, product fulfillment, orders, and other business? Consider what you will need for your office in the way of supplies (including fax machine, computer, desk, chairs, phone, postage meter, pens, and paper) and employees.

- **Insurance:** Consider purchasing general liability insurance, product liability insurance, employee health plans, and any other insurance that pertains to a winery.

- **Financial management:** How will you fund your winery? Do you need to request a loan? What accounting software will you use?

- **Branding your business:** How will you brand your wine bottle labels, business signs, stationery, and Web site? How will you advertise and market your business?

THE FIRST FEW YEARS

Many wineries take years to get started. It may take five years from the time you plant your wines to the time you harvest the grapes and bottle your wine. However, there are other options.

One of these options is to buy grapes from other local wineries. It is important to build good relationships with your competition. Many wineries will sell you some of their grapes to begin making wine while your vineyard matures. In addition, some of the winery owners I spoke with do "custom crush." This means they have the equipment and the room to make wine for another winery. The winery that sells the wine would have a direct part in the creation of the wine, but the wine can be fermented and aged at the winery that offers those services.

Outsourcing services:

"When we first began growing grapes in 1972, we grew them for another winery. It was not until 1988 that we were bonded. In 1990, we opened the winery's doors. We are one of the larger operations in the Yadkin Valley. In fact, we do a custom crush for some of the other local wineries. We process their grapes and create their wine on-site. They then put their label on the wine and sell it at their winery. It is their grapes, and they are an essential part of the process of creating their own wine, we just provide the equipment and space that some smaller wineries do not have when they begin. This also provides another income stream for our business."

— Mark Terry, general manager and winemaker; Westbend Vineyards

Another option is to buy grape juice concentrates. Sometimes this is cost-effective because the concentrates come from large corporate farms, and they can produce the juice for less than it costs a local winery to grow their own grapes. However, this may potentially be an issue with your regional appellation concerning the use of grape concentrates, especially if they come from a different state or country. It could affect some of laws concerning what can be put on a label about where the wine came from. For instance, if a North Carolina winery is buying grape concentrate from California, the North Carolina winery can put on the label that it is a North Carolina wine because the wine was produced there.

If you are a small start-up winery, consider creating wine kits to sell. A couple of the wineries I visited do this. This gets their name on a bottle of wine while they build their vineyard and develop a reputation.

The winery's entertainment value:

"One of the reasons we focused on the beauty and elegance of our tasting room and the grounds is the entertainment value. People cannot afford to jet off to California and visit the grandeur of Napa or Sonoma Valley, but they can drive 15 minutes or even an hour from the city [Winston-Salem] and sit in a beautiful vineyard and sip wine. Bringing people in for the experience of sipping wine in such a romantic environment is a great marketing strategy, as they are more likely to buy cases of wine."

— Steve Shepard, vintner and general manager; RayLen Vineyard & Winery

MARKETING AND ADVERTISING

Try typing in the word "winery" under an Internet search engine, and you will see about 10 million entries. How can your winery compete for exposure? If your winery is in an area saturated with other wineries, you may have trouble even competing on the local level.

Wine and the importance of reputation:

"Listen to your consumers and pay attention to your palate. One of the problems new wineries come across is that even if the wine is bad, they are forced to sell it anyway. This will negatively affect their reputation as a winemaker and also can affect the reputation of other wineries in the region. If it is bad wine, it should not be sold, but I understand that dumping large amounts of wine can sink a winery. They should work carefully with the wine throughout the process to prevent this from happening."

— Steve Shepard, vintner and general manager; RayLen Vineyard & Winery

You must be creative. One way to get your name out there is by entering competitions. If your wines win awards, then display them; let every media outlet you can find know that your wines have won awards. Another way to market your winery is to invite wine critiques to try your wines and write about them in local media outlets. Try to entice even the international critics, such as *Wine Spectator* magazine.

If you do invest in marketing, make sure you know what you are doing, or hire a professional who does. If you have invested thousands of dollars in a winery, do not go cheap when it comes to marketing and advertising, as it can mean the difference between seeing a return on your investment or having the winery close.

Make sure you evaluate your marketing strategies and change them as needed. Create ways for people to critique your business and product; use comment cards and short questionnaires that you send to your customers. This chapter contains ways to bring business to your winery. Remember, there are many people who make wine, so you have to work to attract attention. Most small-to-medium wineries rely on people visiting the tasting room in order to sell cases of wine. Most people pick the cheapest, most convenient wine at the supermarket when they are shopping for dinner. Most of the time, they are not buying cases of wine.

Allison Oaks Vineyards talks distribution and marketing:

"We do our own distribution of our wines. We are a smaller winery, so this is to our advantage. Since we go directly to the wine shops and restaurants, we can sell it at wholesale and make a decent profit. If we used one of the distributors, they would make a part of that profit, and we would either have to raise our prices or find a way for the product to cost less — and we do not want to skimp on quality. This means we are spending a good amount of time getting our name 'out there' and convincing business owners to sell and push our product. We go to different wine events and compete in wine competitions in order to increase our exposure and build confidence in our product."

— Drew Renegar, general manager;
Allison Oaks Vineyards

Bed and breakfasts

Many people who visit local wineries are tourists or people who are looking for an entertaining experience. Therefore, some wineries pair up with local bed and breakfasts or even local restaurants and offer packages in which people can visit the winery or the taste a winery's product served at that location. Some offer weekend packages that might include a bottle or two of wine and a personal tour or dinner at the winery. Check with local establishments because it is a win-win situation for most local businesses, especially ones that rely on tourists.

"When we opened our tasting room, we also included a banquet hall. We do special tasting events and even rent it out. It provides revenue to the business that is necessary to supplement the income from selling wine. We are also supported by the local arts council and do business with a local bed and breakfast."

— Drew Renegar, general manager;
Allison Oaks Vineyards

Winery tours

Many wineries offer tours of their facilities. People get to see how the wine is made and can ask questions of the winemakers. The winemakers, in turn, explain the process and encourage people to taste and buy their specially crafted wines.

If your winery is near other local wineries, it might be a good idea to band together and become part of a "wine trail." You can make brochures that show each winery, what types of wines they produce, a map to their winery, and what the winery hours are. When someone visits your winery, you can suggest that they try to visit the other local wineries. Then, instead of making a trip to just one place, the wine trail becomes a daylong excursion destination, complete with scenery, wine tastings, and maybe even lunch.

One of the wine trails I visited has a punch card. If you buy a wine at a winery, you get a punch on the card. Once you visit all the wineries on the card and have it punched, you can get a free T-shirt that says you completed the wine trail.

Wine trails can be found on the Internet by typing in "wine trails" in a search engine and what area you would like to visit. It would be most convenient if your wineries on the trail have the same hours of business. Some wine trails have special events like live music and art shows, in which all of the wineries participate. In larger areas, they have annual wine festivals complete with bands, local food, activities for the kids, and, you guessed it — wine tasting.

Wine trails with historical importance:

"Our winery is on the Shallow Ford Wine Trail. This trail has a historical significance, as it stretches through the Carolinas as it makes its way from Philadelphia to Georgia. This trail was important during the Revolutionary War and Civil War. There are a number of historic landmarks and places of interest that can be found along the trail. It made sense to have a "wine trail" to coincide with this historical destination, so five wineries are listed on the Shallow Ford Wine Trail to bring more business to all of us. Visit the Web site at **www. shallowfordwinetrail.com**."

— Drew Renegar, general manager; Allison Oaks Vineyards

Wine clubs

Wine clubs are a great way to get people to buy your wine year-round without having to visit the winery. It gives the customers an incentive to buy, as they are able to purchase wine at a discount, and it provides a way for the winery to continually move stock from the shelves.

Westbend Vineyards in North Carolina offers the following to their wine club members. Free membership includes one membership card for two adults (one member and a guest), plus a complimentary Westbend corkscrew as a gift. Upon receiving your first shipment, you may cancel at any time without further obligation.

- No tasting/tour fees

- Discount of 10 percent on all wine purchases and Westbend logo merchandise, and a 20 percent discount on all case purchases

- Quarterly shipments of two to three bottles of preselected wines at a 10 percent discount off retail. Members may pick up shipments at the winery; the cost of wine will vary due to selection and shipping

- Free or discounted admission to select Westbend special events and members- only events

- Refer a friend to join and receive a free bottle of wine in your next shipment

Westbend Vineyards holds a number of events to provide entertainment value to their winery, such as a trip to the Cherokee Casino that is complete with lunch and prizes, wine samplings, red wine, and chocolate. The event includes live music, a candlelit barrel room dinner, a children's hospital benefit, a dinner dance, an educational experience about the making of wine, and more.

In addition to the wine club, Westbend Vineyards also has a new barrel club. This helps offset the cost of some the barrels by having people make a slight investment; in return, they receive:

- A 30-gallon wine barrel personalized with a brass plaque engraved with your name and filled with your choice of Westbend's award-winning barrel-fermented Chardonnay or Merlot

- A free mixed case of wine as a sign-up bonus, plus two cases of wine made from your barrel over the next three years

- Annual Members-Only Gala evening, where you may sample wines from your barrel and others

- No tour or tasting fees at Westbend Vineyards' tasting room

- A 10 percent discount on all wine purchases and Westbend logo merchandise

- A 20 percent discount on case purchases

- Free or discounted admission to select Westbend Vineyards events

Special events

Special events are a great way to get repeat customers to come back to your winery as well as to attract others who may have not chosen to visit in the past. You can have a wine festival like mentioned earlier in this chapter. You can also have new release parties, new wine unveilings, and even crush-and-harvest parties. These can be free events or have a nominal fee. Remember that the goal is to get people to walk out with boxes of wine.

Some wineries have cooking facilities and offer food and wine parings, as well as cooking classes. I visited the Biltmore Estates' winery, and they had an interesting class that pairs wine and chocolate. They place two glasses of wine in front of each person, along with milk chocolate pieces and dark chocolate pieces. The instructor taught the class how to taste, sniff, and view wine. Attendees allowed a piece of the milk chocolate to melt in their mouths as they tried the first wine, then the second. Each person described what it tasted like. At the end of the free demonstration, we got a chance to buy the wines and chocolates used in the demos. It probably cost the winery little, but the memory of my experience is still with me.

Some wineries have packages for weddings, birthdays, anniversaries, or other celebrations. They spend a lot of money on the ambience and setting of the winery. People come because of the beauty and drink, and buy wine while they visit. You can be even more creative and have writers come to sign books, or poetry readers or other artists visit and display their work. Many of the wineries had small shops that not only sold wine, but also local crafts and foods. Whether you just want to make wine as a hobby or as a new business venture, it can be fun and exciting to embark on learning a craft that has fascinated man for centuries. Now you have the basic skills to create a great glass of wine for the fraction of what it costs to buy at a restaurant, and the best part is that you made it with your own two hands.

CASE STUDY:
HOME WINEMAKING
IS MY HOBBY

Richard Schlicht
Home Winemaker
La Crosse, Wisconsin

Richard Schlicht, of La Crosse, Wisconsin, is 79 years old and has been making wine for more than 40 years. Schlicht estimates he has made more than 400 gallons of wine in his spare time. Winemaking is both a hobby and a passion, and Schlicht enjoys giving homemade wine as gifts to his friends and family. He is also happy to show anyone his home winemaking cellar, where you can typically find 40 to 50 gallons of wine in some stage of the fermenting process.

Photo by Jill Stekel
608-553-3536 • Hillsboro, WI

"I have always given wine to my friends and family," Schlicht said. "When my grandson, Greg, got married last summer, I made wine to put on the tables at the reception. My daughter, who is a professional graphic designer, made specials labels for each bottle. I enjoyed being able to do that for my family to make the wedding special."

Schlicht was inspired to make wine because both his parents and grandparents made wine. So when he retired, he found he had more time for his favorite hobby — winemaking. This year alone, he has produced 41 gallons and uses fruits like rhubarb, grape, elderberry, pear, plum, and raspberry. Schlicht uses the book *Bull Cook and Authentic Historical Recipes and Practices*, by by George Leonard Herter and Berthe Herter. This is the book his father gave him, and he still uses it as a reference to this day.

"I enjoy it because it is a wonderful, rewarding hobby," Schlicht said. "On snowy, cold days I like to bottle wine. I work on wine for months at a time. I don't have a license, but I like to give my wine way to friends and family. Of course, I like to drink it too."

Richard Schlicht displays the wine he is currently fermenting in glass jugs

Schlicht with homemade wine he has made and bottled

Crocks used to create homemade wine

Schlicht's wine labels

APPENDIX A

Wine Yeast Strains

There are many different types of yeast strains you can purchase. Keep in mind that the name of the yeast strain refers to the type of grape from which they were harvested. The yeast strains that are created in laboratories usually have a number associated with them. The column with the heading Alcohol Tolerance refers to the highest percentage of alcohol in the wine that the yeast can withstand before they begin to die off.

Dry yeast packets

Name	Brand	Type of Wine	Alcohol Tolerance
Narbonne 71B-1122	Lavlin	white/blush	14%
Champagne EC-1118	Lavlin	cider, late harvest, stuck fermentations, sparkling	18%
Montpellier K1V-1116	Lavlin	fruit wines	18%
Red Wine RC-212	Lavlin	red, berry	12% to 14%

Name	Brand	Type of Wine	Alcohol Tolerance
White Wine ICV-D-47	Lavlin	white, rose, mead	15%
Montrachet	Red Star	all-purpose, vegetable, grain	13%
Premier Cuvee	Red Star	white, melons	18%
Pasteur Champagne	Red Star	sparkling, mead	15%
Cote des Blancs	Red Star	orchard fruits, white	14%
Red Pasteur	Red Star	red, berries	16%
Saccharomyces Cerevisiae AW4	Vintner's Harvest	dry white wines	14.5%
Saccharomyces Cerevisiae BV7	Vintner's Harvest	sweeter white wines	13%
Saccharomyces Bayanus CL23	Vintner's Harvest	blush, dry, citrus	18%
Saccharomyces Cerevisiae CR51	Vintner's Harvest	red, berries	13.5%
Saccharomyces Cerevisiae CY17	Vintner's Harvest	fruit wines, blush	15%
Saccharomyces Cerevisiae MA33	Vintner's Harvest	fruit wines, blush, herbal, grain	14%
Saccharomyces Cerevisiae R56	Vintner's Harvest	Zinfandel, light-tasting fruit wines	13.5%
Saccharomyces Cerevisiae SN9	Vintner's Harvest	aged wines, pit wines, berries	18%
Saccharomyces Cerevisiae VR21	Vintner's Harvest	red, berries, fruit	15%

Liquid yeast

Liquid yeasts come in packets or test tubes and are either activated yeast or have an activator that has to be broken inside the packet. These are faster and more reliable yeast packets, but also cost $5 or more, compared to about $1 for a dry yeast packet.

Name	Brand	Type of Wine	Alcohol Tolerance
Champagne	White Labs	sparkling, strawberry, raspberry	17%
Avise Wine Yeast	White Labs	mixed white, pear, peach, grapefruit	15%
Sweet Mead and Wine	White Labs	dandelion, mead, fruit, plum	15%
Steinberg-Geisenheim Wine Yeast	White Labs	dandelion, light fruit, root	14%
Chardonnay White Wine	White Labs	white, light fruit, herb	14%
French White Wine Yeast	White Labs	white, mead, rice, grain	16%
Merlot Red Wine Yeast	White Labs	red, berry, heavy red fruit	18%
Assmanshausen Wine Yeast	White Labs	blush, mixed, strawberry, berry	16%
French Red Wine Yeast	White Labs	red, berry, heavy red, fruit	17%
Cabernet Red Wine Yeast	White Labs	heavy red, chocolate, vegetable	16%
Suremain Burgundy Wine Yeast	White Labs	pit, red	16%
English Cider	White Labs	apples, pit, mead, grain	14.00%
Pasteur Champagne	Wyeast	sparkling, Champagne, strawberry, raspberry	17%
Chateau Red	Wyeast	cherry, berry, red	14%
Sake #9	Wyeast	mead, rice, grain, plum, sake	16.00%
Sweet Mead	Wyeast	mead, pit, seeded	11%
Chablis	Wyeast	fruity whites	12%
Chianti	Wyeast	cherry, berry, red	14.00%
Bordeaux	Wyeast	red, heavy fruit	14%

Name	Brand	Type of Wine	Alcohol Tolerance
Eau de Vie	Wyeast	barleywine, high alcohol red	21%
Dry Mead	Wyeast	herb, cyser, mead, fruit mead	18%
Cider	Wyeast	apple, peach, cherry, mead	12%
Port wine	Wyeast	heavy red, cherry, raspberry, blue-berry	14%
Rudesheimer	Wyeast	ice wines, meads, sweet cider	12%
Zinfandel	Wyeast	high-sugar fruit	18%

Types of mead and different ingredients

Name of Mead	Ingredients
Simple mead	Contains honey; there may be other ingredients such as citrus fruit, but these are added to raise the acid level, rather than be a major component of flavor
Sack mead	Contains extra honey, although may contain other ingredients as well
Melomels	Fruit
Metheglins	Herbs and spices
Rhodamels	Flowers
Rhizamels	Vegetables
Pyment	Grape juice
Braggot	Hops
Black mead	Black currants
Capsicumel	Chile peppers
Cyser	Apple juice
Morat	Mulberries

Conversion Chart for Specific Gravity / Brix / Percent ABV

Brix or Balling	Specific Gravity	Potential Alcohol
6.0	1.0236	3.3%
7.0	1.0277	3.9%
8.0	1.0317	4.4%
9.0	1.0359	5.0%
10.0	1.0400	5.5%
11.0	1.0441	6.1%
12.0	1.0483	6.7%
12.5	1.0504	6.9%
13.0	1.0525	7.2%
13.5	1.0546	7.4%
14.0	1.0567	7.7%
14.5	1.0589	8.0%

Brix or Balling	Specific Gravity	Potential Alcohol
15.0	1.0610	8.3%
15.5	1.0631	8.5%
16.0	1.0653	8.8%
16.5	1.0674	9.1%
17.0	1.0697	9.4%
17.5	1.0719	9.6%
18.0	1.0740	9.9%
18.5	1.0762	10.2%
19.0	1.0784	10.5%
19.5	1.0806	10.7%
20.0	1.0828	10.9%
20.5	1.0851	11.3%
21.0	1.0873	11.6%
21.5	1.0895	11.9%
22.0	1.0918	12.1%
22.5	1.0941	12.4%
23.0	1.0964	12.7%
23.5	1.0986	13.0%
24.0	1.1009	13.3%
24.5	1.1032	13.5%

Wine With Food

Pairing wine with food:

"It is important to pair the right wine with a meal. The food should not overwhelm the wine. Simple food goes well with a great wine. If the meal is too heavy it can overtake a wine. My mother told me that two pieces of jewelry is enough; you should not overdo it. And the same is true of food and wine. Food and wine should complement one another, not compete."

— Eileen Crane, president and winemaker; Domaine Carneros

Pair red wines with:

Beaujolais: strong cheese*, pasta (red sauce), appetizers, poultry, and pork

Pinot Noir: pork, beef, strong cheese*, and pasta (red sauce)

Merlot: chocolate, beef, pasta (red sauce), and strong cheese*

Cabernet: chocolate, beef, pasta (red sauce), and strong cheese*

Zinfandel: beef, pasta (red sauce), and strong cheese*

Port: chocolate or strong cheese*

*= Brie (ripe), Camembert, Blue Castello, Oregon Blue, Pipo Crem, Danish Blue, Roquefort, Gorgonzola, Stilton, Chevre Crescenza, Pont l'Eveque, Port du Salut, Taleggio, Beer Cheese, Esrom, Limburger, Munster (Alsatian), Oka, Emmenthaler, Fontal, Fontina d'Acosta, Cheddar (sharp), Feta, Parmigiano Reggiano, Pecorino

Pair white wines with:

Chenin Blanc: mild cheese, strong cheese, appetizers, shrimp, crab, lobster, shellfish, Asian food, and poultry

Sauvignon Blanc: mild cheese, strong cheese, appetizers, shrimp, crab, lobster, shellfish, poultry, oysters, and seafood with light sauce

Gewürztraminer: mild cheese, appetizers, Asian food, poultry, and pork

Dry Riesling: mild cheese, strong cheese, appetizers, shrimp, crab, lobster, poultry, seafood with light sauce, and grilled fish

Chardonnay: strong cheese, appetizers, oysters, seafood with light sauce, grilled fish, and seafood with cream sauce

White Riesling: chocolate or mild cheese

APPENDIX D

Resources

WEB SITES

The Northern Brewer Homebrew Forum: **http://forum.northern brewer.com**

More Flavor! Inc.; More Wine!: **http://morewinemaking.com**

The Winemaking Home Page: **www.winemaking.jackkeller.net**

WineBusiness.com: **www.winebusiness.com**

Napa Fermentation Supplies: **www.napafermentation.com**

E.C. Kraus Home Wine & Beer Making Supplies: **www.eckraus.com**

Seven Bridges Cooperative: **www.breworganic.com**

Midwest Homebrewing and Winemaking Supplies: **www.midwestsupplies.com**

GLOSSARY

Aging: Allowing wine to sit in a cool place for six months to a year to improve the taste. This is sometimes done in oak barrels.

Airlock/Fermentation Lock: This is a device that allows carbon dioxide to be released from a vessel without allowing oxygen to get into the wine.

Autolysis: This is the process of yeast breaking down the sediment in a fermentation vessel. It can lead to off-flavors in a wine.

Campden Tablet: This is a tablet that contains potassium metabisulfate. It is used to sterilize wine.

Cap: This is formed when fruit floats to the top of a must and is then punched down during early fermentation.

Bentonite: A type of clay used for clearing, or fining, a wine.

Brix: This is a measure on a hydrometer that calculates percentage of sugar in a wine. It is used to calculate the potential alcohol that a wine must may produce. Brix is measured in degrees or as a percentage.

Carboy: This is a glass jug that comes in different sizes and is usually used during secondary fermentation.

Dry: This is a term to describe when all the sugars have been fermented. It is the opposite of sweet.

Fermentation: This is the process that wine undergoes as live yeast transforms sugars into two main by-products: CO_2 gas and ethyl alcohol.

Free Run Wine (Vin de Goutte): This is the wine created by maceration before pressing.

Hydrometer: This is an instrument that measures the specific gravity or density of a wine.

Isinglass: This is a type of fining agent that is made from the parts of a sturgeon.

Lactic Acid: This is a type of acid that is naturally found in grapes. It is also created during the process of malolactic fermentation in which malic acid is transformed into lactic acid.

Lees: These are dead yeasts that form a type of sludge at the bottom of a fermenter. Usually, the wine is racked off these lees because leaving them can impart negative flavors in a finished wine.

Maceration: This is the technique of extracting phenols, namely tannins, from grape solids in red wines. This process adds color, flavor, and body to a red wine.

Malic Acid: This is a natural acid found in grapes and wine. It can impart a green grass flavor to wine in higher concentrations. This can give wine a harsh taste. Malic acid is necessary in the maturation of grapes on the vine.

Malolactic Fermentation (MLF): This is the process that a wine will undergo that transforms harsh malic acid into a milder lactic acid. This process is important to smooth out the flavor.

Must: This is the term for a juice that is fermenting before it becomes a wine.

Oxidation: This is what occurs when wine is exposed to oxygen. This is one of the main causes of spoiled wine. Oxygen is important to start a healthy fermentation, but too much exposure can lead to oxidation. This can also turn wines a brown color.

pH: The level of acidity in wine. It can be tested with an acid testing kit and be adjusted by adding different acids, such as citric acid or acid blends. If the wine is too acidic, a base should be added or the must diluted. The pH of a wine is important in color, flavor, fermentation, and the aging of a wine. The pH measures the hydrogen ion concentration in a wine.

Pitch Yeast: This is the act of adding yeast to a wine must.

Pomace: The name of wine solids left after maceration.

Press Wine (Vin de Presse): This is the wine that is extracted from the pomace after maceration. Depending on the winemaker's taste or the local habit, free-run wine and press wine are blended or treated separately.

Potential Alcohol: This is a measure of how much alcohol can be produced in a wine, if all of the available sugar is used. This is higher than the actual alcohol content of a wine because there is usually some residual sugar left for taste. Potential alcohol is calculated using the Brix, or percentage of sugar present in the wine multiplied by 0.55, which is the percentage of alcohol produced by yeast when metabolizing sugar.

Racking: This is the act of siphoning clear wine off lees in a carboy. This process helps clear a wine by leaving particles behind. It sometimes takes a few different rackings to get a wine totally clear.

Sparkling: Wine that has bubbles, like Champagne.

Specific Gravity: This is a measure of the ratio of the weight of volume of a wine compared to water. This can be measured using a hydrometer and is similar to the Brix of a wine, because sugar makes a solution more dense.

Still Wine: Wine that has no bubbles.

Stuck Wine: This is when fermentation has stopped.

Sweet Wine: This is the opposite of dry wine and contains at least 3 percent sugar after it has fermented.

Tartaric Acid: This is an acid that is naturally found in grapes in higher concentrations. Tartaric acid is responsible for the flavor, tartness, and color of a wine. Sometimes tartaric acid is not fully soluble in wine and will form crystals that resemble shards of glass. These can be removed through cold stabilization.

Total Acidity: This is referred to as titratable acid, or TA. This is a measurement of the total percentage of acid in a wine and is not the same thing as pH, which is the strength of the acid in a wine. It is usually expressed as grams per liter and can be tested using a titration method of adding a alkaline solution until the sample has been neutralized.

Tannin: This is contained in the skins of grapes and gives wine astringency.

Vintage: This is the year grapes are harvested, not the year a wine is bottled.

BIBLIOGRAPHY

Books and articles used:

Cox, J. *From Vines to Wines, The Complete Guide to Growing Grapes and Making Your Own Wine*. Maine: Storey Books. 1999.

Jackisch, Phillip. *Modern Winemaking*, Ithaca: Cornell University Press. 1985.

Marie, D. *Wild Wines, Creating Organic Wines from Nature's Garden*. NY: Square One. 2008.

Peynaud, Emile. *Knowing and Making Wine* (English Translation). Wiley-Interscience. 1984.

Proulx, A., Nichols, l. *Cider Making, Using and Enjoying Sweet and Hard Cider*. Maine: Storey Publishing. 2003.

Spaziani, G. *The Home Winemaker's Companion, Secrets, Recipes, and Know-how for Making 115 Great-Tasting Wines*. Maine: Storey Publishing. 2000.

Spence, P. *Mad About Mead*, St. Paul: Llewellyn Worldwide. 1997.

Vargas, P., Gulling, R. *Making Wild Wines and Meads, 125 Unusual Recipes Using Herbs, Fruits, Flowers and More*. Maine: Storey Publishing. 1999.

WineMaker Beginner's Guide, 2004, *WineMaker Magazine*.

Web sites used:

Got Mead: Your Mead Resource: **www.gotmead.com.**

Penn Museum, The University of Pennsylvania Museum of Archeology and Anthropology: **www.museum.upenn.edu/new/exhibits/online_exhibits/wine/wineintro.html.**

Roxanne's Wine Cellar: **http://scorpius.spaceports.com/~goodwine.**

Dan Meyer's Web site: **http://blue-n-gold.com/halfdan/meadrecp.htm.**

Washington Winemaker Blog: **www.washingtonwinemaker.com.**

Talisman Farms: **www.talisman.com/mead.**

Winepress Forum on Winemaking: **www.winepress.us.**

Drink Nation: A site of drink recipes: **www.drinknation.com.**

Wine Intro with Lisa Shea: **www.wineintro.com/quotes/songs.**

AUTHOR BIO

John was born in Miami, Florida, in 1970. He grew up in the Tampa Bay area but attended the North Carolina School of the Arts, in Winston Salem, for high school. He attended Florida State University and earned a bachelor's degree in psychology from Appalachian State University. He finished his master's degree and Ph.D. in natural health at Clayton College of Natural Health in spring 2002. In August 2007, he took the plunge. John had been a social worker in child protective services for far too many years but had been toying with the idea of being a writer. He had written for a few national magazines and had received positive responses for his work. He decided to quit social work and took a chance at writing full-time. Luck was on his side, as during his first year, he was assigned to write seven books for Atlantic Publishing Group, Inc. Since then, he has completed numerous freelance projects, including writing for magazines, and creating workbooks, e-books, articles, blogs, ghost-written books, and much more. He is now working full-time, and hopes to get some fiction completed and published soon. More information can be found at **http://johnperagine. books.officelive.com**.

INDEX